# On Foot Guides

# London

D0129393

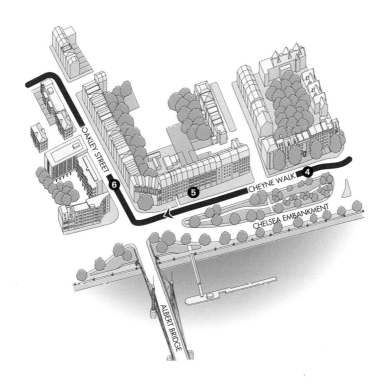

ON FOOT GUIDES

# LONDON WALKS

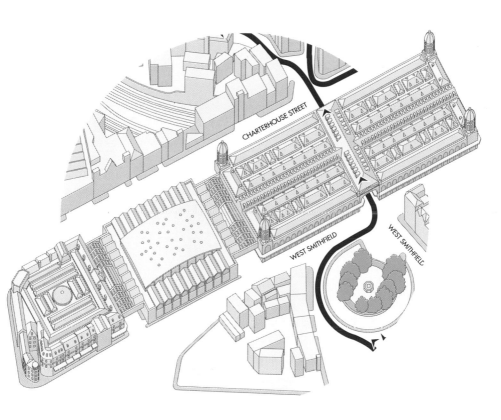

## Second Edition

## Celia Woolfrey

DUNCAN PETERSEN

**INSIDERS'** GUIDE®

GUILFORD, CONNECTICUT
AN IMPRINT OF THE GLOBE PEQUOT PRESS

Copyright © 2000 Celia Woolfrey
Copyright © 2001, 2006 Duncan Petersen Publishing Ltd

This updated edition published 2006 by:
Duncan Petersen Publishing Limited
C7, Old Imperial Laundry
Warriner Gardens, London SW11 4XW
United Kingdom

Published in the USA by:
The Globe Pequot Press, LLC
P.O. Box 480
Guilford, CT 06437
Insiders' Guide is a registered trademark of The Globe Pequot Press.

Sales representation and distribution in the U.K. and Ireland by Portfolio Books Limited
Unit 5, Perivale Industrial Park
Horsenden Lane South
Greenford UB6 7RL
Tel: 0208 997 9000

Duncan Petersen ISBN–13: 978-1-903301-46-3
Duncan Petersen ISBN–10: 1-903301-46-7
Globe Pequot ISBN–13: 978-0-7627-4161-8
Globe Pequot ISBN–10: 0-7627-4161-9

Conceived, designed and produced by
Duncan Petersen Publishing Ltd

**Editorial Director** Andrew Duncan
**Editors** Fiona Duncan, Leonie Glass and Hermione Edwards
**Art Director** Mel Petersen **Designers** Christopher Foley and Ian Midson
**Maps** Andrew Green

Printed by: Delo-Tiskarna, Slovenia

# Visit Duncan Petersen's travel website at
## www.charmingsmallhotels.co.uk

# CONTENTS

# Exploring London on foot

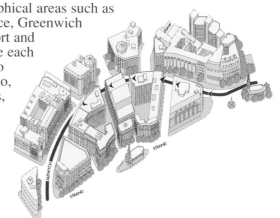

Although London is not a compact city, it's marvellous for walking. Perhaps this is because of its many separate neighbourhoods. Many of these were former villages which merged together as the city grew, but still retained their often highly distinctive character. In a city that reached its prime before the days of motor transport, walking is also, naturally, the most effective way to see and learn about London. The walks in this book are designed to show you the city in all its facets – great monuments as well as hidden nooks and crannies – and to give a taste of a Londoner's London.

The aerial-view – isometric – mapping used to illustrate our 15 walks makes this guide the perfect companion as you explore the city. Streets, parks, squares, even individual buildings are brought to life on the page. There is no need for full directions – the route as marked on these maps is very easy to follow, and the numerals link to information about places of interest in the text.

Our walks, based on geographical areas such as Chelsea, St Paul's, Little Venice, Greenwich and so on, are deliberately short and mostly compact, around a mile each in length. They are designed to encompass plenty to see and do, including interesting museums, art galleries, shops, restaurants, pubs and cafés. Depending on how often you stop, a walk could take you all day to complete, or just a morning – or less.

---

### HOW THE MAPPING WAS MADE

The mapping used in this book was originally created from specially commissioned photographs taken from a helicopter which flew at about 1,500 feet, with the camera angled at 45°. Weather conditions had to be slightly overcast in order to achieve a maximum level of detail on the buildings.

Scores of enlargements were made from negatives, which a group of technical illustrators then used to create the maps, working in pen and ink. For this book, the mapping has been developed further: extracted areas have been digitally redrawn and coloured.

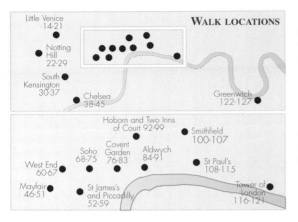

Numerals on the maps correspond to the numerals in the text, highlighting places of interest and importance. Where a specific building is highlighted, the numeral will appear on the building, but where there are several places of interest in the same street, the numeral will normally be placed on the street. The text reference to the place of interest appears in bold print, which is also used to highlight other significant places nearby – buildings, museums, galleries, statues, sculptures, restaurants, cafés or shops. Where relevant, opening times are given for sights so that you can organize and time your walk (for more information on admissions to sights, see page 13).

## HOW TO USE THIS BOOK

The area covered by the walks is bounded by Little Venice in the north, Greenwich in the south and east and Notting Hill in the west.

### Using the maps

The route taken by each walk is clearly marked on the map with the occasional arrow to ensure that you keep heading in the right direction. Boxes tell you where the walk starts and finishes and where the nearest tube stations are – generally not more than a few minutes' walk away.

## WHEN TO USE THIS BOOK

Most of the walks can be enjoyed at any time of the year, but some – especially those just out of the centre and those in areas with a vibrant street life – are obviously much more fun to walk when the weather is fine.

## LINKING THE WALKS

The *Chelsea* walk can be linked neatly to *South Kensington* if you walk north up Sydney Street, cross the Fulham Road and then continue up Sydney Place (which becomes Onslow Square) to South Kensington tube station.

The *St James's and Piccadilly* walk ends at Piccadilly Circus, where the *West End* and *Soho* walks begin, so you could combine it with either of these or with *Mayfair,* which starts at Half Moon Street near Green Park tube station, a few hundred metres to the west along Piccadilly.

The *Soho* walk ends at Leicester Square, the starting point of the *Covent Garden* walk.

Covent Garden could also be linked with *Aldwych* if you backtrack to Wellington Street and the Strand, or by tube with *Holborn and Two Inns of Court* (Covent Garden is one stop from Holborn on the Piccadilly line).

At the end of the *Aldwych* walk, you could head north up Kingsway to the start of *Holborn and Two Inns of Court.* This walk could also be combined by foot with *Smithfield,* starting at Farringdon, and by tube with *St Paul's,* which starts at Bank (Holborn is three stops from Bank on the Central Line).

## SUMMER WALKS

**CHELSEA:** if you want to visit the Chelsea Physic Garden, it's only open between mid-April and mid-October (for days see page 41).

**COVENT GARDEN:** an area which acquires a continental feel when the sun shines, drawing the street performers to the Piazza and encouraging the restaurants and cafés to set tables and chairs on the pavements outside.

**LITTLE VENICE:** this walk can end with a boat trip to Regent's Park or Camden Lock, a potentially chilly experience in winter when the boats only run at weekends; in the summer you have much more choice as they run hourly every day of the week.

**NOTTING HILL:** pick a sunny Saturday if you want to browse in Portobello Road's open-air antiques market.

**TOWER OF LONDON:** the views are what makes this walk special so, though you could do it at any time of the year, make sure you have a bright day.

**GREENWICH:** fine weather is really a prerequisite for enjoying this walk through stunning parkland and Greenwich 'town'.

## WINTER WALKS

**LITTLE VENICE:** recommended as a summer walk if you finish up with a boat trip; but the canals look beautiful in winter too, and you'll avoid the crowds.

**MAYFAIR:** you can take refuge from the cold and the rain in Burlington Arcade and then, if the movie appeals to you, while away a few hours in the comfort and warmth of the Curzon cinema.

**SMITHFIELD:** within a stone's throw of the covered market, traditional cafes and trendy bars serve hearty breakfasts (some serve from 6am) and hot soup to set you up against the cold.

**SOUTH KENSINGTON:** a perfect walk for winter, South Kensington includes the Victoria and Albert, Natural History and Science Museums.

## WEEKEND WALKS

**COVENT GARDEN:** the atmosphere is more relaxed at the weekend, when there's almost continuous street theatre and people come here just to have fun.

**NOTTING HILL:** Portobello Road antiques market – an important element of this walk – is only held on Saturday; or come here over the August bank holiday weekend (the last in August) when the Notting Hill Carnival takes place.

## WEEKDAY WALKS

**ALDWYCH:** this walk takes you into the heart of the Middle and Inner Temples, which are only open to the public between Monday and Friday.

**HOLBORN AND TWO INNS OF COURT:** Gray's Inn Chapel and Gardens are only open from noon to 2.30pm Monday to Friday.

**ST PAUL'S:** a part of the City that buzzes during the week; but at weekends, restaurants and some shops are closed – even on Saturday – and the streets can be eerily deserted.

**WEST END:** Regent and Oxford Streets are always busy, but the crowds are worse at weekends and unbearable in the days leading up to Christmas – so avoid these times if possible.

**SMITHFIELD:** the meat market is only held from Monday to Friday; and as business starts at the crack of dawn, start your walk early.

## WALKS FOR KIDS

The following walks could be especially enjoyable for children: **Tower of London,** fitting in visits to the Crown Jewels and the armouries (if the queues aren't too long) and the Tower Bridge Experience; **Covent Garden,** including a visit to the Transport Museum; **South Kensington,** taking in the Natural History and Science Museums; **Little Venice,** ending the walk with a narrowboat trip; and **Greenwich,** with a visit to the Cutty Sark and Gypsy Moth.

## GETTING AROUND
### THE TUBE

All our walks have been devised with a convenient tube station in mind. The nearest station to the start and end is indicated on each walk.

The London Underground network is extensive, efficient, and a fast way of getting about the city. There is, however, still room for improvement. Tube stations are by and large depressing, and trains are often overcrowded, especially at rush hour. A notable exception is the extension of the Jubilee Line, from Green Park to Stratford, with new stations such as Southwark, Bermondsey, Canada Water and Canary Wharf worth a visit in themselves. Another recent innovation has been the overland Docklands Light Railway (DLR) linking the City with Docklands.

### Using the tube

Each tube station is on at least one of nine Underground lines. Each line is designated by a colour on tube maps displayed in stations and on trains, and available at information points. In central London particularly, a station may be served by several lines, and this makes it easy to change from one line to another. To plan your route; (and where you should, if necessary, change trains) simply follow the lines from your departure station to your destination. Trains run daily from around 5.30am (7.30am on Sunday) to around midnight.

Stations are identified at street level by the London Transport symbol – a red circle cut by a blue horizontal line. Tickets can be bought at machines, or if you are in doubt, from the ticket office, where you should state your destination. Keep your ticket until it is collected by hand, or, more usually, by an automatic gate, at the end of your journey.

### Tube fares

The tube system is divided into six zones, and depending on how many zones you need to cross on a particular journey, the fare increases accordingly. With the exception of Little Venice and Greenwich, all the walks in this book are in Zone 1.

There are several different types of ticket, all explained in the *Fares and Tickets* booklet available at information points in tube stations, or phone London Travel Information on 020 7222 1234, or visit the website www.tfl.gov.uk. You have several ticketing options: a single or return ticket for one journey at a time, Carnet Tickets (a book of 10 single tickets valid for zone 1) or an Oyster card (adding money to it as you go). Also available are Travelcards (one, three or seven day; one month; and Family) for use on tubes, buses, DLR and on the rail network within London.

### LONDON BUSES

'Just hop on a bus' may seem a rather daunting epithet to first-time visitors to London faced with the complex route system. In reality, the system is fairly

---

### THE WEATHER

English weather is rarely given to extremes, but it is unpredictable and can change character several times a day. It is a constant and characteristic topic of British conversation. Average daytime temperatures range from 6°C (43°F) in winter (Dec-Feb) to 21°C (70°F) in summer (June-Aug), only occasionally going below 0°C (32°F) or above 27°C (80°F). The temperature in London is generally mild, but a combination of wind and damp air can make it seem cold. There is an annual rainfall of 60cm, most of it falls in winter. Visit the website www.bbc.co.uk/weather for forecast information.

straightforward, and cheaper and more fun than the tube, though much slower. That said, getting around on a bus in Zone 1 should be quicker than when we first published in 2000, due to the congestion charge (now charged to all cars driving in central London). How much difference this has made, however, is debatable. Red double-decker buses and single-decker 'hopper' buses, each displaying a number, run along correspondingly numbered routes. Bus maps showing routes are available from information points.

The timing of buses can be somewhat erratic (timetables displayed at bus stops should not be relied on) and buses are notorious for appearing in groups of three after a long interval. Bus stops display the numbers of the buses which call there. If the stop has the word 'request', the bus will only halt if a passenger on the bus rings the bell, or someone at the stop raises their hand. The conductor (or, on some buses, the driver) will collect your fare; the amount varies on how far you are travelling, although on some buses you cannot pay on board. For details of bus fares, see the booklet *Fares and Tickets* available at information points. Buses run from about 5am to anything up to 1am, with night buses on selected routes. All major night bus routes pass through Trafalgar Square.

Some buses stop short of the end of their route. Look at the front of the bus as it approaches in order to see where it is destined to stop, and check that it is going far enough for you; other people in the queue will usually help.

**London Transport information points**
London Transport Information Centres are located at the following places:

• Euston Station
• King's Cross Station
• Liverpool Street Station
• Oxford Circus tube station
• Victoria tube station
• Piccadilly tube station
• St James's tube station
• Heathrow Central tube station
• Heathrow, Terminals One, Two, Three and Four

## TAXIS
Londoners who find themselves in foreign cities such as New York are usually terrified by the indigenous taxi drivers, who appear to have scant regard either for traffic regulations or for human life. By contrast, London cabbies are superb drivers, and neither they nor their stately black taxis are given to flashy manoeuvres. They also know their way around town and have had to pass an exam on the subject, known as 'the knowledge'. If you are not at a taxi stand (outside stations, large stores etc), you can hail a taxi in the street, if its yellow 'For Hire' sign above the windscreen is illuminated. The fare is shown on the meter. You should add a 10-15 percent tip, though to save time, cabbies prefer it if you simply round up the fare and say "keep the change". Sometimes drivers can be difficult about taking their 'fares' to destinations to which they don't want to go; remember that they are obliged to take you if the destination is within six miles of the pick-up point.

If you wish to order a taxi by phone, there are several numbers to call:
Computer Cab    Tel. 020 7286 0286
Radio Taxis    Tel. 020 7272 0272
Dial-a-Cab    Tel. 020 7253 5000

At certain times of day, phoning for a minicab (usually an ordinary car) may be more economical. Most minicabs don't have meters, so the fare must be agreed on at the start of the trip. However, they can occasionally be unreliable, and finding your destination may prove a problem. The following company is reliable:
Addison Lee    Tel. 020 7387 8888

## TOURIST INFORMATION

Tourist information centres are located at:

1 Regent Street, Piccadilly Circus (Britain Visitor Centre: open Mon-Fri 9.30am-6.30pm, Sat-Sun 10am-4pm; Jun-Oct Sat-Sun 9am-5pm).

Liverpool Street underground station (open Oct-May 8am-6pm, Jun-Sep 8am-7pm).

Heathrow Airport, terminals 1, 2 and 3, underground station concourse (open Jun-Sep 8am-7pm, Oct-May 8am-6pm).

Greenwich, Pepys House, 2 Cutty Sark Gardens (open daily 10-5).

Waterloo International Terminal, Arrivals Hall (open 8am-10.30pm).

There is also a Corporation of London information office opposite the south side of St Paul's Cathedral (open 9.30am-5pm; Tel. 020 7332 1456).

Royal Naval College

For more information, telephone Visit London on 0870 1566 366 or visit the website www.visitlondon.com.

## USEFUL TELEPHONE NUMBERS

### Disabled visitors

Disabled visitors can receive guidance from the Disabled Information service run by RADAR (Royal Association for Disability and Rehabilitation) on 020 7250 3222, or from Artsline on 020 7388 2227.

### Sightseeing tours

London Transport's double-decker Original London Sightseeing Tour bus takes visitors on four different tours, departing every 12 minutes daily between 8.30am and 7pm. The main starting points are Victoria Street, Marble Arch, Baker Street, Embankment Pier and Haymarket, but there are 90 stops and 20 interchange points along the way. Tickets can be bought on the bus (cut-price, direct-entry tickets to Madame Tussaud's also included). The original circular tour lasts one and a half hours; buses are open-topped in summer (for more information, call 020 8877 1722 or visit the website www.theoriginaltour.com). Most luxurious is the Harrods half- or full-day tour, also with an eight-language commentary (Tel. 020 7225 6596). Apart from Harrods, several other companies offer luxury coach tours, with stop-offs for guided visits round London's principal sights, or for river-boat cruises, such as: Golden Tours (also known as Frames Rickards), 123-151 Buckingham Palace Road, SW1 (Tel. 020 7233 7030).

### River trips

Boats run frequently every day from Westminster and Charing Cross piers to the Tower and Greenwich (contact City Cruises on 020 7930 9033 and Greenwich Riverboats on 020 7930 4097), and in summer, further downstream to the Thames Barrier and upstream to Kew or Hampton Court. For further information, fares and departure times, visit the website www.tfl.gov.uk or ask for the leaflet 'Thames River Services' at information points.

### London Eye

For a bird's eye view of London, one of the city's most recent major tourist attractions is the British Airways London Eye, on the south bank opposite Big Ben. For

ST PAUL'S CHURCHYARD

information and booking, Tel. 0870 500 0600. You can collect pre-booked tickets or buy them direct from County Hall (next to the Eye), where you can also hire binoculars and leave luggage. There is access for disabled visitors.

**Theater tickets**
You can pre-book tickets through Ticketmaster by visiting the website www.ticketmaster.com. Alternatively, there is an excellent half-price ticket booth in Leicester Square (open Mon-Sat noon to 6.30pm, Sun noon to 3.30pm). To find out what's on – not just theater, but film, dance, clubs, exhibitions, etc. – buy *Time Out* (published weekly), *TNT* (a free magazine which you can pick up on the street), *Hot Tickets* (a magazine that comes with the Thursday edition of the *Evening Standard* newspaper), or the Saturday edition of the *Guardian*.

**Admissions and opening times**
The London Pass saves you money on entrance fees to many of London's top museums, galleries and other attractions, and includes discounts on theater tickets. Visit the website www.londonpass.com for more information.

A recent development is free admission to

---

**EMERGENCY INFORMATION**

For Police, Ambulance or Fire dial 999 or 112 from any phone. No coins are needed. The operator will ask which service you require.

**Hospitals with 24-hour casualty (emergency) departments:**
Charing Cross Hospital, Fulham Palace Rd, W6
Tel. 020 8383 0000.
St Mary's Hospital, Praed St, W2
Tel. 020 7886 6666
Royal Free Hospital, Pond St, NW3
Tel. 020 7794 0500
St Thomas' Hospital, Lambeth Palace Rd, SE1
Tel. 020 7188 7188

**Late-opening pharmacies**
Chemists operate a duty rotation for evenings and Sunday so that one chemist in each area will be open at these times; rosters are posted in chemists' windows. There is just one 24-hour pharmacy in London, Zafash, which is located near Earl's Court at 233-235 Old Brompton Road (Tel. 020 7373 2798).

the general collections of the Victoria and Albert Museum, the Natural History Museum and the Science Museum, though a fee is charged for their temporary exhibitions.

**Left luggage and lost property**

If you can't face heaving your bags around with you, a central telephone number will advise on which railway stations have left luggage facilities (Tel. 020 7486 2496). Call the same number for lost property if you have left something on an overground train. If you have lost property on a tube train or bus, visit or telephone the London Transport Office at 200 Baker Street, NW1 (recorded information on 020 7486 2496).

Cutty Sark Gardens

KING WILLIAM WALK

**SHOPPING AND BANKING HOURS**

Generally speaking, shops in central London are open between 9 or 9.30am and 5 to 6pm, from Monday to Saturday. Fashion and gift shops may not open until 10am. Since the relaxation of the Sunday trading laws, many shops are now open on Sunday, although the hours are shorter (often from 11am to 5pm). Most central London shops stay open one evening a week for 'late-night' shopping. Oxford Street shops stay open until 8pm on Thursday; Knightsbridge and King's Road shops stay open until 7pm on Wednesday. Certain chains of food stores have very late opening hours, as well as some small corner shops. Giant supermarkets such as Sainsbury's stay open at least until 8pm; on some nights as late as 10pm; and some branches are open all night on Friday.

From Monday to Friday banks are open from 9.30am; some close at 5.30pm, others earlier. Some bank branches open on Saturday. In the centre, they include Barclays at 30 Sloane Square, SW3 (open 10am-2pm) and 208 Kensington High

Street, W8 (open 9am-3pm), and Lloyds at 399 Oxford Street, W1 (open 9.30am-3.30pm).

Bureaux de change (poorer exchange rates than banks) have longer opening hours and can be found at airports and stations, as well as in some tube stations and main shopping streets. There are several 24-hour bureaux de change, for example Chequepoint at Marble Arch, Earl's Court Road and Queensway.

**PUBLIC HOLIDAYS**

On the following days of the year it feels like a Sunday, with banks and many shops closed: New Year's Day (1 Jan), Good Friday, Easter Monday, May Day (first Mon in May), Spring Bank Holiday (last Mon in May), August Bank Holiday (last Mon in Aug), Christmas Day (25 Dec) and Boxing Day (26 Dec).

---

**WALKING SAFELY**

Although Londoners often ignore them, it is advisable to use zebra or pelican crossings, where pedestrians have priority, or underpasses. A few outer areas are unsafe for pedestrians after nightfall: if outside the city centre after dark, stick to the well-lit main streets.

# Little Venice

Colourful narrowboats and white stucco-clad houses line the basin of the Regent's Canal in the area known as Little Venice just north of Paddington. This walk is fun to do in summer or at a weekend when the waterway is at its busiest. In winter the area takes on a more peaceful beauty – your quiet stroll will only be interrupted by bird calls, the hum of distant traffic and ducks scooting along the glassy water. To extend the circuit, you can take one of the narrow-boat cruises which travel from Little Venice to Regent's Park and Camden Lock Market. Or with an A-Z mapbook, you can follow towpaths and backstreets and do the same journey by foot.

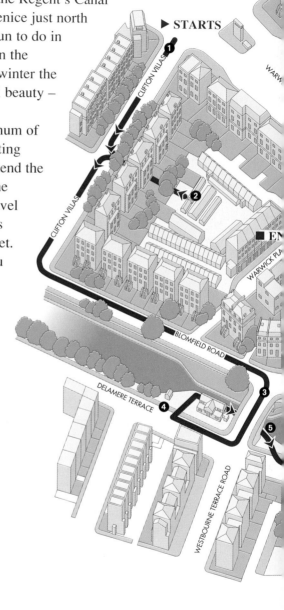

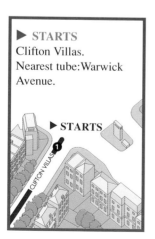

▶ **STARTS**
Clifton Villas.
Nearest tube: Warwick Avenue.

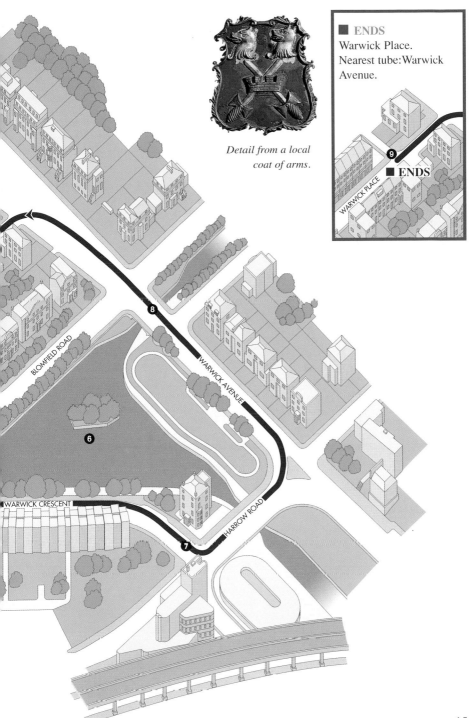

**■ ENDS**
Warwick Place.
Nearest tube: Warwick
Avenue.

*Detail from a local*
*coat of arms.*

■ ENDS

WARWICK PLACE

BLOMFIELD ROAD

WARWICK AVENUE

WARWICK CRESCENT

HARROW ROAD

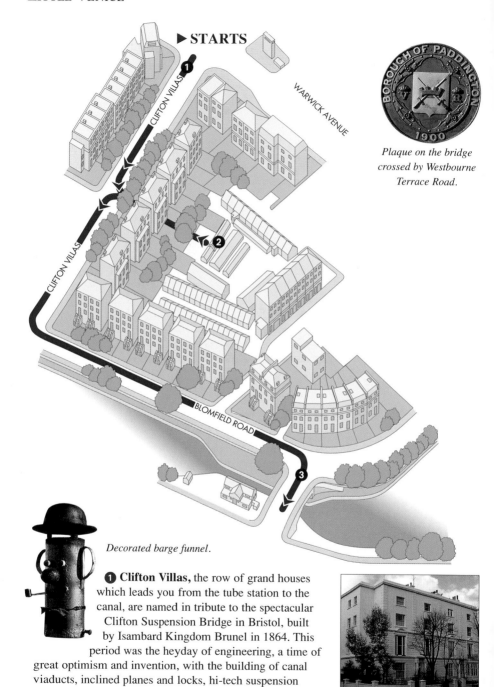

Plaque on the bridge
crossed by Westbourne
Terrace Road.

Decorated barge funnel.

❶ **Clifton Villas,** the row of grand houses
which leads you from the tube station to the
canal, are named in tribute to the spectacular
Clifton Suspension Bridge in Bristol, built
by Isambard Kingdom Brunel in 1864. This
period was the heyday of engineering, a time of
great optimism and invention, with the building of canal
viaducts, inclined planes and locks, hi-tech suspension
bridges, and iron passenger ships. Before the age of the
railways, most of Britain's freight (both raw materials and
finished products) was carried inland on a vast network of

White stuccoed houses of
Clifton Villas.

canals. Little Venice was part of a large-scale local development. As excavators dug out Regent's Canal, home builders kept pace. When completed, the waterway linked the Grand Union Canal with the heart of London and continued east to the Limehouse docks along the Thames.

*There has been a pub on the site of the Bridge House since the days when Westbourne was a village.*

❷ Little Venice is better known now for its leafiness and tranquillity, despite its connections with the Industrial Revolution. It is a residential area of smart houses and formal gardens, many of them stocked with plants from **Clifton Nurseries** halfway along Clifton Villas. It may not be the cheapest place to buy spiky 'architectural' plants, clipped topiary and olive trees, but the selection is huge. Alongside the outdoor nursery there's a steamy glasshouse with a wide range of orchids and exotic houseplants, plus pots to suit every whim, from antique urns to oriental planters.

*Above and right: garden sculptures from Clifton Nurseries.*

❸ Turn left along **Blomfield Road,** a street lined with grand, white stuccoed houses. The canal is hidden at this point by a high wall, and you get your first glimpse of it as you head towards the bridge at Westbourne Terrace Road. On the corner is the **Bridge House** pub, occupying one of the first Georgian houses to be built after the Regent's Canal was finished in 1812. It was built on the site of an alehouse, which served ploughmen and farmers when the area was surrounded by farmland and part of the village of Westbourne. Upstairs is the **Canal Café Theatre,** well-established on the London fringe, with a long-running satirical 'News Revue' worth catching (Thur-Sun).

*Narrow boats are typically decorated with elaborate lettering and designs.*

# LITTLE VENICE

*Narrow boats moored in the*
*Little Venice Basin.*

④ As you stand with your back
to the Bridge House pub, the
section of canal in front of you is an
extension of the Grand Union, built to link
Paddington and the West End with the
expanding industrial areas around
Birmingham. The canal was built during a
time of great upheaval, and two pioneering
figures who embodied the spirit of the age
lived in **Delamere Terrace** behind you.
Edmund Gosse, chronicler of the late 19th
century in his novel *Fathers and Sons* was a
resident here, followed later by Edmund
Wilson, artist, surgeon and crew member of
the *Discovery* on Scott's voyage to
Antarctica.

*Former*
*tollhouse next to*
*Warwick Terrace*
*Road bridge.*

**5** A turn along the towpath under the bridge (wide enough for the horses pulling narrow boats to pass through) takes you past the **London Waterside Café** – a floating café and information centre. (Tel. 020 7482 2550 for information about boats to Camden Lock and London Zoo.) Along the boat ride is the **Maida Hill Tunnel,** which boatmen used to have to 'leg' their way through by lying on their backs on top of their boat, and 'walking' their way along the tunnel ceiling while their horses were led over the top.

**6** The Grand Union links with the Regent's Canal at the **Little Venice Basin,** sometimes known as Browning's Pond, named after the poet Robert Browning who lived here after the death of his wife in Florence in 1861. Browning is credited with coining the term Little Venice, although others say that it didn't take off until real estate agents, keen to talk up prices in the area, started using it in the 20th century. Browning's house at 19 Warwick Crescent was pulled down in the 1960s to make way for an apartment block.

WESTMINSTER CITY COUNCIL
ROBERT
BROWNING
POET
1812 – 1889
LIVED IN
WARWICK CRESCENT
1862 – 1887
THE ARMSTRONG BROWNING LIBRARY

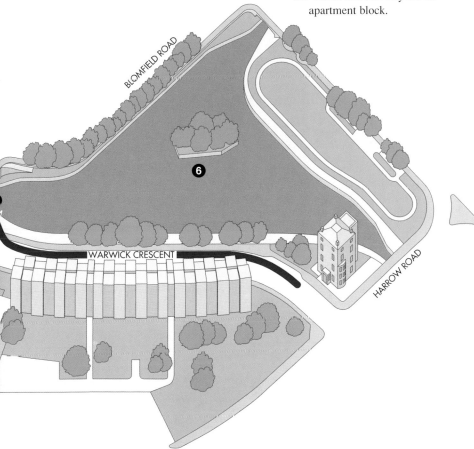

**7** The reality of northwest London hits as you reach the end of Warwick Crescent. If you turn your back momentarily on the calm canal basin, you are confronted with the raised section of the road, built in the 1960s, that carries much of the city's traffic to the west. Underneath it runs **Harrow Road,** laid down over the route of an old Celtic track and once the main street down to Paddington. At the corner, **2 Warwick Crescent,** now used as offices, was once a boarding house for musicians where the short-story writer Katherine Mansfield lived for a while in the early 1900s.

**8** Head over the bridge and skirt **Rembrandt Gardens** on **Warwick Avenue.** Another bridge takes you across the canal and back into Blomfield Road. Narrowboats travelling this canal work their way downhill via 12 locks before reaching the River Thames at Limehouse. On the way they pass old warehouses with great arched windows and red brick façades, architectural relics of the canal age. Some have been converted into loft-style apartments; another near King's Cross (off the map) has been turned into the **London Canal Museum** (12 New Wharf Road; Tel. 020 7713 0836). It was built in the 1860s for Carlo Gatti, a famous ice-cream maker of the time. Inside, the museum tells the story of life on the canals and the trade in natural ice before the days of refrigeration.

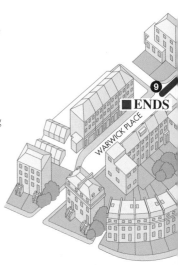

**ENDS**

**9** A cut-through to Warwick Place brings you back to the **Clifton Nurseries** shop at No. 3, selling garden ornaments and statuary, obelisks, urns and amphorae. If you're in need of refreshment at the end of this walk, there are two choices: the pub next door, the **Warwick Castle,** or the **Green Olive** restaurant at No. 5 (Tel. 020 7289 2469), serving robust modern Italian cuisine.

*In the late 18th and early 19th centuries it was possible to travel by narrowboat from the Thames to Liverpool docks and from Bristol to Leeds.*

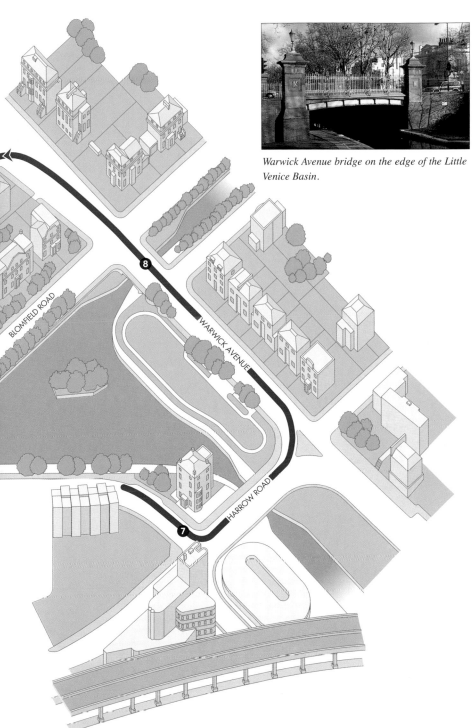

*Warwick Avenue bridge on the edge of the Little Venice Basin.*

BLOMFIELD ROAD

WARWICK AVENUE

HARROW ROAD

8

7

# Notting Hill

*Street art, Notting Hill.*

The weekend is the best time for a trip to Notting Hill, when market stalls fill most of Portobello Road, starting with antiques, curios and junk at the Chepstow Villas end and culminating in fruit and vegetables near the Westway (off our map). Saturday is the day for antiques, and there's a clothes market near the Westway on Friday. During the week the fruit and veg market is open Monday to Saturday, although it is closed on Thursday afternoon. Numerous small shops specializing in interior design, retro clothes, books and records are open and there are plenty of bars and restaurants in the area worth seeking out too. If you are in London on the August bank holiday weekend, Notting Hill Carnival, Europe's biggest street party, is always an experience not to be missed. Each year around a million visitors pack the streets, dancing in front of pulsating sound systems, or admiring the feather-clad dancers and steel bands sailing past costume parade floats.

The area has been through some peaks and troughs since the mid-1800s, when property developers hastily built many of the white stucco houses for workers at nearby potteries and pig farms. The overcrowded area fell into poverty and many of the houses in the northern part of Notting Hill were eventually subdivided into tenements. In the 1950s and

1960s, huge numbers of immigrants from Trinidad and Barbados gravitated towards Notting Hill, followed by so-called 'trustafarians' – middle class youngsters with trust funds – in the 1980s and 1990s.

▶ **STARTS**
Kensington Church Street. Nearest tube: Notting Hill Gate. At the tube station follow the signs for Kensington Church Street.

■ **ENDS**
Pembridge Gardens. Nearest tube: Notting Hill Gate.

NOTE: to get the most out of this walk continue along Portobello Road (off the map) for the market (weekends) and return to pick up the route at stage 6.

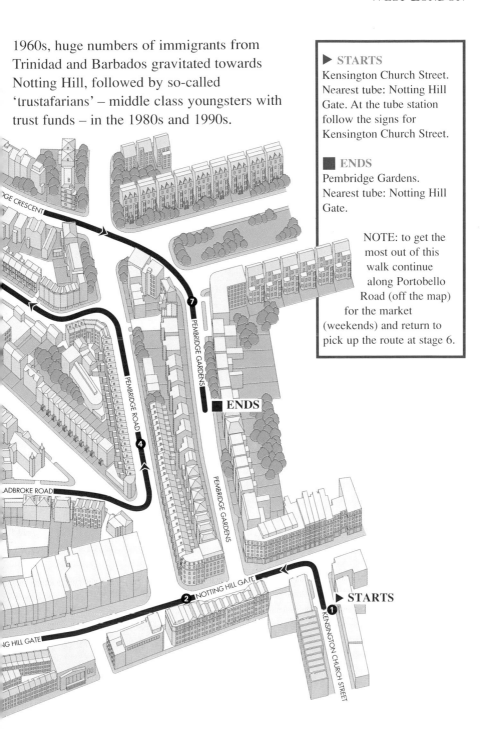

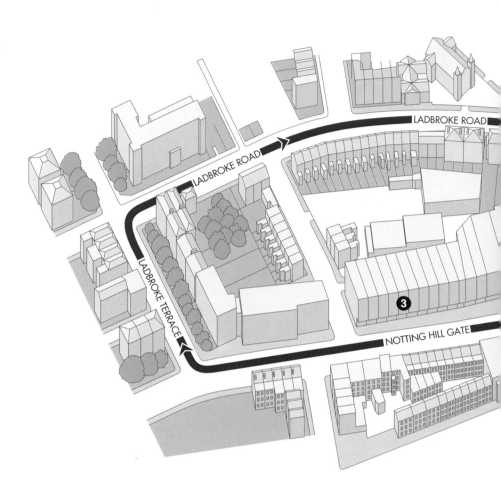

❶ Notting Hill is sophisticated on its Kensington borders, with several upscale restaurants on Kensington Church Street, such as the fashionable restaurant **Kensington Place** at 201-207 (Tel. 020 7727 3184). Reasonable value (by London standards), especially at lunchtime, it has an appealing fish counter. This is a well-healed part of town – you'll see people carrying yoga mats, scurrying to a class, or browsing in the fine art and antiques shops such as **Denton Antiques** (partner shop of **Mrs M.E. Crick**), who specialise in chandeliers from 1750-1900. The display window is a marvel.

*Kensington Place.*

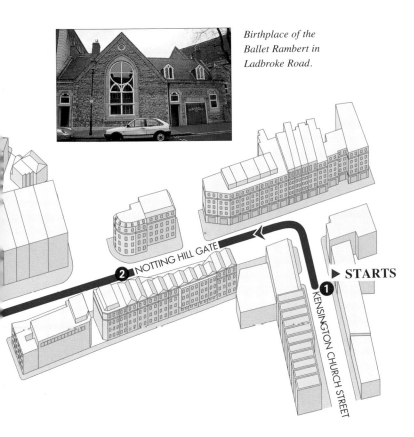

*Birthplace of the Ballet Rambert in Ladbroke Road.*

**2** **Notting Hill Gate** is more workaday with its **Book and Comic Exchange,** old-style fishmongers **Chalmers and Gray,** and **The Gate,** a repertory cinema showing films other than the usual Hollywood offerings. The cream-and-coral façade of the **Coronet Cinema** is by W.G.R. Sprague who also designed the interior in similarly ornate Louis XVI style. Originally the Gaumont Theatre, Sarah Bernhardt and Ellen Terry were among the actors who played there.

**3** In the 1700s and 1800s, Notting Hill Gate was little more than a tollgate surrounded by cottages and coaching inns. By the end of the 19th century the area began to change. The urban poor arrived,

living in cramped, squalid cottages rented by unscrupulous landlords. Little more than 100 years later, these terraced houses are highly sought-after, despite extremely high price tags.

On Campden Hill Road, is the popular Windsor Castle pub with its wood panelled interiors and olde worlde atmosphere.

*The Windsor Castle.*

**4** You have now left Notting Hill Gate via Ladbroke Terrace and Ladbroke Road, named after James Weller Ladbroke who developed the 'garden city' north of Notting Hill Gate. Cross the road, veering left into Pembridge Road, past a busy parade of shops. Continue to the top end of **Portobello Road,** usually packed with people heading for the antiques market on Saturdays with a few cars trying to push their way through the crowds. Among the antique shops and galleries on this part of Portobello Road is the delectable **Hummingbird Bakery** (No. 133). Its cupcakes are not to be missed. Worth browsing in are **Retro Home** at 30 Pembridge Road for second hand furniture and *objets*, with clothes at **Retro Woman and Retro Man** respectively at 32 and 34 Pembridge Road. **Caira Mandaglio** at 31 Pembridge Road sells quirky interior design in impeccable taste. A few doors down at No. 41, **Visto** offers 1950s china and accessories.

### CARNIVAL

Notting Hill carnival started as a street party for children from a local adventure playground in 1964 and didn't become the huge festival it is now until the 1970s. Carnival is now a commercial event, with many more outsiders than Notting Hill-ites attending, and though there were incidents of violence in the 1970s and 1980s, these days things are much calmer. Carnival takes place over the last weekend in August. Sunday is given over to the children's costume parades. Monday is a much more frenetic affair, with adult steel bands, dancers, a big parade and sound systems all competing for cash prizes. As far as music goes, there's still some soca – the indigenous music of Trinidad – to be heard. Played by steel drum bands, Soca originates from the days when drums were banned by plantation owners. Musicians had to make do with the pots, pans and tin cans available to them, later finding ways to fine-tune the hammered tops of disused oil drums to create the tones they desired. The traditional sounds of the Caribbean are mixed with every style of contemporary black music as towering piles of speakers compete with other body-vibrating sound systems nearby. Then there's the crush of people – you have to go with the flow. Take time out if you find a stall selling street food, or home-made rum punch, that appeals. The main Carnival route winds for 5 km (three miles) along Ladbroke Grove, Westbourne Grove, Chepstow Road and the Great Western Road but the smaller streets in between are packed with sound systems, stalls and live bands too. *Time Out*, the *Caribbean Times* and *The Voice* are good sources of information of what happens when. One final thing to bear in mind is that public transport is the only way to get here (the nearest tube stations are Royal Oak, Westbourne Park and Notting Hill Gate) but Ladbroke Grove tube station is closed for the duration of Carnival weekend.

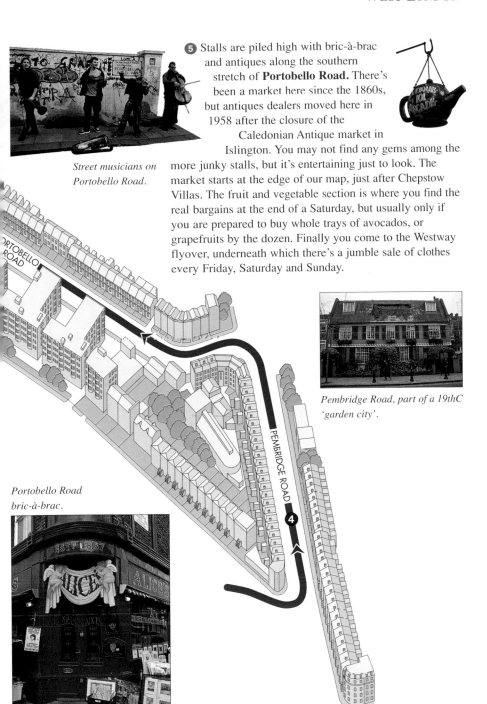

**5** Stalls are piled high with bric-à-brac and antiques along the southern stretch of **Portobello Road.** There's been a market here since the 1860s, but antiques dealers moved here in 1958 after the closure of the Caledonian Antique market in Islington. You may not find any gems among the more junky stalls, but it's entertaining just to look. The market starts at the edge of our map, just after Chepstow Villas. The fruit and vegetable section is where you find the real bargains at the end of a Saturday, but usually only if you are prepared to buy whole trays of avocados, or grapefruits by the dozen. Finally you come to the Westway flyover, underneath which there's a jumble sale of clothes every Friday, Saturday and Sunday.

*Street musicians on Portobello Road.*

*Pembridge Road, part of a 19thC 'garden city'.*

*Portobello Road bric-à-brac.*

**❻ Chepstow Villas** and the streets between there and Pembridge Square were part of the Victorian housing development built by James Weller Ladbroke. Garden squares, proper drainage systems and churches were all part of the 'model' scheme, put up to entice new residents to the area. Other street names, such as Kensington Park Road, were chosen for their upmarket, green and leafy connotations. Ladbroke rented some land to a local man, John Whyte, to build a racecourse around Ladbroke Grove, using Notting Hill as a natural grandstand. The course, known as the Hippodrome, was not a success as the ground was rough and made racing dangerous, and jockeys refused to ride there. The horse traders striking their deals near the course were the unwitting forerunners of Portobello Road market.

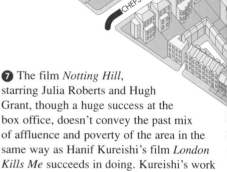

**❼** The film *Notting Hill*, starring Julia Roberts and Hugh Grant, though a huge success at the box office, doesn't convey the past mix of affluence and poverty of the area in the same way as Hanif Kureishi's film *London Kills Me* succeeds in doing. Kureishi's work was much more open about the fact that the residents of streets like **Pembridge Gardens** and those nearby were the wealthy tip of an iceberg, with poverty and crime not far below the surface, though these days gentrification is pretty much complete.

*Typical housing in the area.*

---

### WHERE TO EAT AND DRINK

**Market Bar,** 240a Portobello Road (Tel. 020 7229 6472). Thai restaurant upstairs, bar downstairs with a good mix of people.

**Beat Bar,** 265 Portobello Road (Tel. 020 7792 2043). Music bar at the Ladbroke Grove tube station end of Portobello Road. Strong on hip hop and funk, serving cocktails called Extreme Shots along with beer and wine.

**Trailer Happiness,** 177 Portobello Road (Tel. 020 7727 2700). A kitschy haven of trailer park glamour, with Southwest

American cuisine. Nearest tube: Ladbroke Grove.

**Ground Floor,** 186 Portobello Road (Tel. 020 7243 8701). A popular bar with big sofas, a good atmosphere and a beer garden. Wines and Belgian beers, and modern European cooking. Nearest tube: Ladbroke Grove.

**Notting Hill Arts Club,** 21 Notting Hill Gate (Tel. 020 7460 4459). A wide-ranging crowd packs into this no-frills, grungey, garage-like basement bar, that is a great place to dance to a diverse mix of world

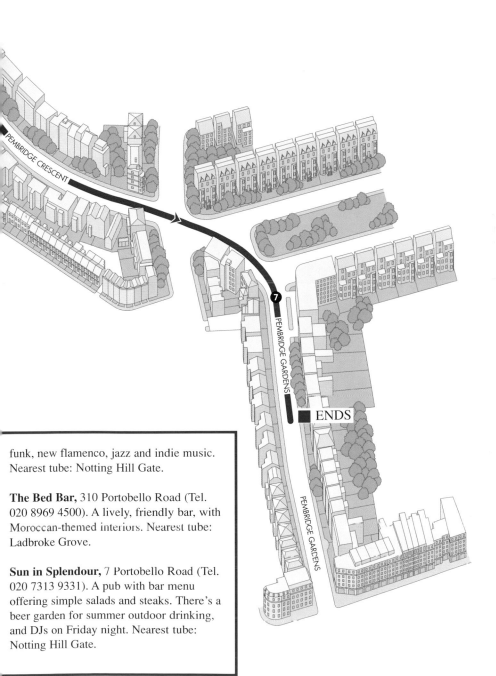

ENDS

funk, new flamenco, jazz and indie music.
Nearest tube: Notting Hill Gate.

**The Bed Bar,** 310 Portobello Road (Tel.
020 8969 4500). A lively, friendly bar, with
Moroccan-themed interiors. Nearest tube:
Ladbroke Grove.

**Sun in Splendour,** 7 Portobello Road (Tel.
020 7313 9331). A pub with bar menu
offering simple salads and steaks. There's a
beer garden for summer outdoor drinking,
and DJs on Friday night. Nearest tube:
Notting Hill Gate.

# South Kensington

► **STARTS**
Exhibition Road. Nearest tube: South Kensington. If you want to skip stage 1 of the walk, follow the signs at the tube station for the 'Museums' exit.

► **STARTS**

*Detail from the façade of Alfred Waterhouse's Natural History Museum.*

I f every area has a defining moment then South Kensington's came in the 1850s when Prince Albert, consort to Queen Victoria, proposed a Great Exhibition in a crystal palace in Hyde Park – a project for which he was widely derided. In 1851 the exhibition went ahead nonetheless and was a huge success, with six million visitors producing enough profit to buy a tract of land stretching from Kensington Gardens to the Cromwell Road. On these 87 acres museums and learned institutions sprang up, each holding the prime collections of their kind in the world. These have now evolved into the Natural History Museum, the Science Museum and the Victoria and Albert Museum (commonly known as the V&A). Far from stuffy Victorian institutions, these museums have kept up with the times, going out of their way to appeal to children.

■ **ENDS**
Albert Memorial, Kensington Gardens. Nearest tube: Knightsbridge or South Kensington.

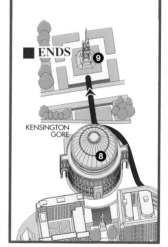

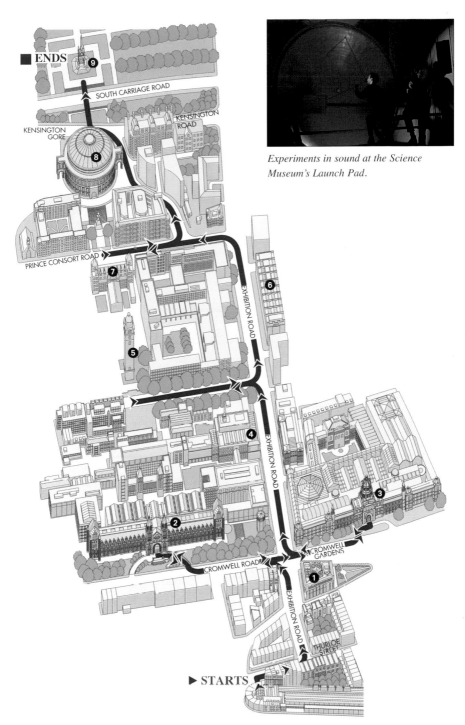

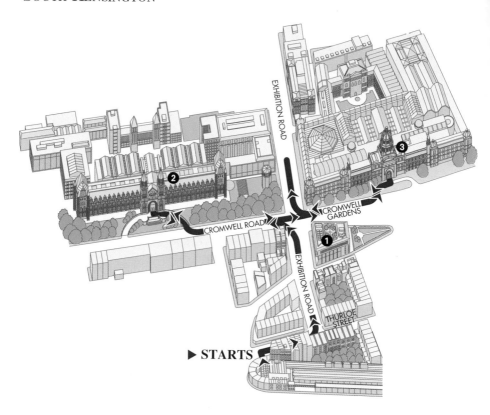

**1** The discount fine art and science books in the shops around **Thurloe Street** are among the first signs that you are approaching London's Museum Mile. It's a good idea at this point to pick out the highlights of the museums you want to investigate. These can be overwhelming places, requiring return visits to do them justice.

As you reach the Cromwell Road, the geometrical, granite-faced building on the corner is the **Ismaili Centre** (1983) designed for London's Ismaili Muslim community by Hugh Casson and Karl Schlamminger. The interior has the reflective and sparkling surfaces, flat planes and lightness of colour of Islamic tradition. Though the building is open to the public on guided tours only once a month, a glimpse of the geometric entrance hall with its quietly bubbling fountain

reveals the architectural themes beyond. For pre-museum snacks, **Daquise,** the café at 20 Thurloe Street, is recommended for its *barszcz* with *ushka* (clear beetroot soup with wild mushroom ravioli), *blinis* with smoked salmon, and other no-nonsense Polish food.

**2** 'Kids go free' is the slogan of the **Natural History Museum,** and its displays – dinosaurs hatching out of their eggs or eating one other, an earthquake in a Japanese supermarket, an erupting volcano, a gallery called Creepy Crawlies and a zoo of stuffed mammals including a lion you can stroke – pull in the crowds daily. There are two entrances: to the Life Galleries on Cromwell Road, and to the Earth Galleries on Exhibition Road. The museum aims to show science in action, with plenty on ecology, human health and the complex

*The brick and terracotta Natural History Museum (1881).*

Raphael cartoons; sculpture from India; and Japanese and Chinese art and ceramics. As a museum it has been influential, prompting the re-evaluation of the 'English' applied arts, such as the work of genius wood carver Grinling Gibbons. A fine example of his work is the limewood cravat (c.1690) carved to look so much like Venetian lace that Earl Horrace Walpole once wore it when greeting French visitors at his home in Strawberry Hill. He reported that 'the French servants stared and firmly believed that this was the dress of English country gentlemen.' (Open daily 10am-5.45pm; 10am-10pm Wed and last Friday of each month.)

interconnection of the natural world. The museum's 300 scientists moved into the new £27 million Darwin wing in 2000, and the museum now has at least 90 percent of its collection on display – an impressive achievement for an enterprise that receives 100 new specimens from the reefs and rainforests of the world for every hour it is open. (Open Mon-Sat 10am-5.50pm; Sun 11am-5.50pm.)

❸ True to the 'improving' theme of its time, the **Victoria and Albert Museum** was established to shake up British design. The core of the collection was bought up from the Great Exhibition of 1851, showcasing the best of what were known back then as the 'industrial arts' from the Empire and beyond. A Punch cartoon of the era shows a family gazing quizzically at the exhibits on show – among them a 16thC serving dish wriggling with glazed earthenware eels, salamanders, an escaping lobster and a frog by Bernard Palissy. This exhibit can still be seen in the museum. It's an eclectic collection – its former director Roy Strong described the V&A as "an extremely capacious handbag." Among the highlights are the Canon Photography Gallery; the textiles and dress collections including 20thC fashion; paintings by Constable;

*Right: Michelangelo's David in the Italian Cast Court*

*Below: The Cromwell Road façade of the Victoria & Albert Museum, a labryrinthine building by Aston Webb (1890).*

**4** In the **Science Museum,** one look at the scorched, tin-foil covered Apollo 10 command module immediately raises the question: how could such a flimsy craft make it through the earth's atmosphere, all the way to the moon, and then get back to earth in one piece? The museum is an inspiring place, but not just on subjects like space travel – it manages to make complex technical subjects such as the discovery of the structure of DNA exciting and accessible too. This is another vast knowledge bank: the museum recommends that you start at the top and work your way down, unless you are with 3-6 or 7-11 year olds, in which case head for the basement, where they will enjoy The Garden. The excellent interactive Launch Pad gallery of experiments is for children of all ages. There is also an IMAX cinema. (Open daily 10am-5.45pm.)

**5** To get to the **Queen's Tower,** walk onto the Imperial College campus via Imperial College Road, almost opposite Princes Gardens. Amidst this block of 1960s-era labs and a library is this elusive tower, whose foundation stone was laid by Queen Victoria, 'Empress of India' in 1887. Unfortunately the tower is now closed to the public, and its bird's-eye views are exclusively enjoyed by the great and the good on official visits.

*Science Museum: Apollo 10 command module.*

**6** Across Exhibition Road at No. 55, the **Polish Hearth Club** (Ognisko Polskie) was set up for Polish airmen in 1940, and drinking at the padded vinyl bar puts one in the company of a portrait gallery of khaki-clad World War II commanders. The vodka, kept ice-cold, is served by the thimbleful to a clientele ranging from businessmen to the occasional priest. The service is extremely welcoming. The club is a centre for the now dwindling Polish community, but the restaurant is open to everyone (Tel. 020 7589 4635). On the menu are herring with sour cream, roast goose with celeriac and potato dumplings, hunter's stew and lamb *shashlik*.

*Queen's Tower,*
*unfortunately now*
*closed to the public.*

**7** A few steps past the triumphal arch entrance of Imperial College brings you to the **Royal College of Music,** one of the world's leading conservatories. Students hang out on the steps outside during term time, and free concerts are offered here all year. Its museum of historic instruments is open on Wednesdays and Thursdays in term time, from 2-4.30pm (special visits by appointment, free admission or £5 for a guided tour. Tel. 020 7591 4346; Fax 020 7589 7740).

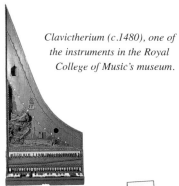

*Clavictherium (c.1480), one of the instruments in the Royal College of Music's museum.*

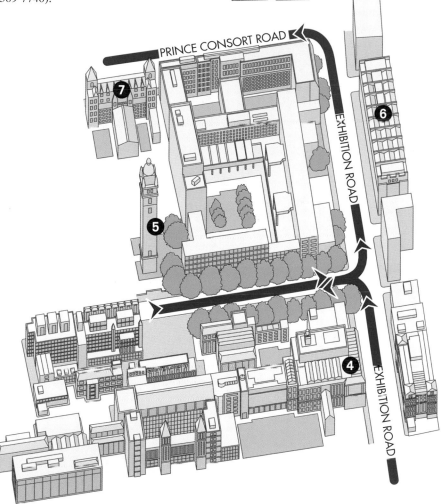

**8** A canyon of red-brick mansion blocks on either side of Albert Court funnel you towards the **Royal Albert Hall.** The beautiful, glass and iron-domed landmark, completed in 1870 by engineers Fowke and Scott, was lit originally by lime-light lamps, whose lime cylinders were raised by flame to a white heat. The Albert Hall is best known as the venue for the summer promenade concerts, or Proms, popular because if you are prepared to stand, ticket prices can be affordable. The acoustics of the hall are often criticized though these, and the ventilation, have been improved in recent building work.

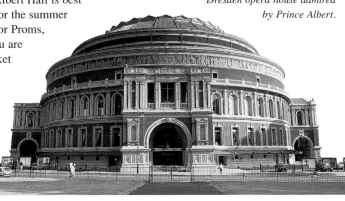

*Royal Albert Hall, based on a Dresden opera house admired by Prince Albert.*

**9** Recently restored, the **Albert Memorial** (1876) by George Gilbert Scott is glorious, ornate and unfashionable in a world that loves minimalism and would prefer to forget its colonial past. The figures clustered around Prince Albert – an elephant (Asia), ox (Europe), bison (America) and camel (Africa) – represent the world's dominions. Commerce and agriculture are glorified here, along with an all-gold Albert, beloved consort of Queen Victoria, who built the shrine to him 'for a life devoted to public good'. The figure of Albert holding a catalogue from the Great Exhibition of 1851 is like a gilded Buddha, sheltered by a canopy encrusted with mosaics, enamels and 'jewels'. In case the modest Albert might seem too much in focus, the whole lot is topped by choirs of gilded angels, raising their arms gospel-style, and a huge cross.

*Prince Albert stated in vain that he "would rather not be made the prominent feature" of a monument.*

### FOOD

This is not a walk to be attempted on an empty stomach. As well as the museum cafés, there are some interesting pit-stops around South Kensington tube station, including Carluccio's at 1 Old Brompton Road, a café-deli with a menu of inspiring Italian food, and good either for a quick bite or a full meal. Bibendum, off the map at 81 Fulham Road, serves light lunches and evening drinks in the art deco mosaic-clad foyer of the former Michelin Tyre Co. HQ. There are also cheaper French cafés and bistrots on the Old Brompton Road, such as **La Bouchée** at No. 56, a cheerful French eatery.

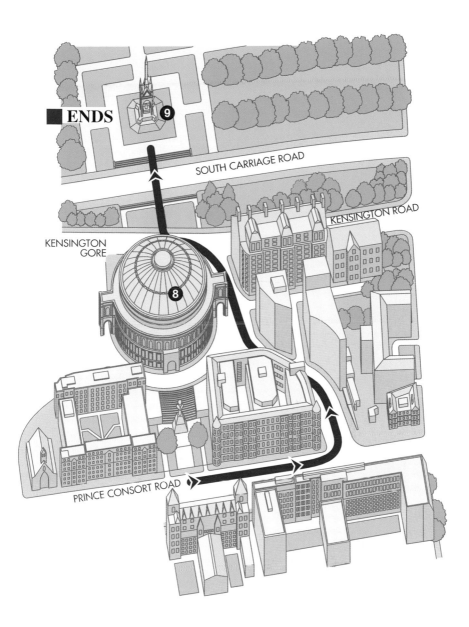

ENDS ⑨

SOUTH CARRIAGE ROAD

KENSINGTON ROAD

KENSINGTON GORE

⑧

PRINCE CONSORT ROAD

# Chelsea

Fashionable King's Road is Chelsea's main focus. But between the King's Road and the river is old Chelsea, the key to the area's bohemian roots. A stroll along Tite Street takes you past the former homes of some rebellious 19thC artists, Whistler among them. "He made London a half-way house between New York and Paris", according to Max Beerbohm, "and wrote rude things in the visitors' book." The route passes Cheyne Walk, site of Henry VIII's 16thC manor house. By this time the area attracted so many aristocrats that it was nicknamed Village of Palaces, although it began life as a humble fishing village.

▶ STARTS
Royal Hospital Road and Tite Street. Nearest tube: Sloane Square. Turn left out of Sloane Square tube station and walk along Lower Sloane Street. At Royal Hospital Road, turn right and keep walking until you reach Tite Street, a ten minute walk.

■ ENDS
King's Road at Bramerton Street. Nearest tube: South Kensington or Sloane Square.

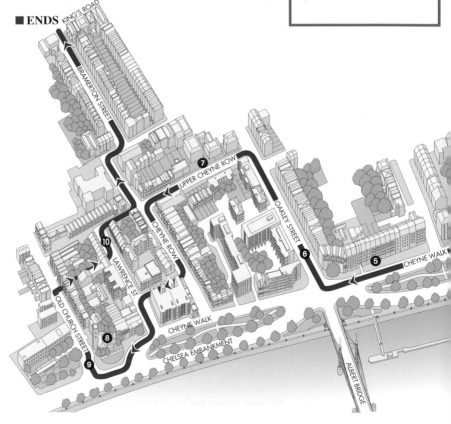

Boatyards, potteries and alehouses were pulled down to make way for the new Embankment.

*Chelsea Embankment: The Boy David, a memorial to First World War machine gunners.*

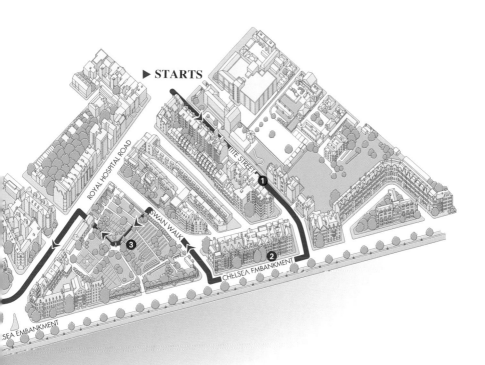

▶ **STARTS**

*Chelsea Embankment gardens: A memorial to the Sixth Dragoon Guards and their part in the South African War of 1899-1902.*

## Whistler v. Ruskin

Whistler had to sell his White House almost as soon as it had been built to pay off his legal debts after a court case against the art critic John Ruskin. Their argument summed up the clash of old and new in the arts at the time. Ruskin criticized Whistler for asking 200 guineas for his painting *Nocturne in Black and Gold: the Falling Rocket* calling it "Cockney impudence", and saying that it was the equivalent of the artist "flinging a pot of paint in the public's face." Whistler took Ruskin to court for libel and won, but was awarded only a farthing in damages. As a result Whistler was bankrupted and left England for Venice to recoup his fortunes.

❶ **Tite Street** was the hub of the radical new art world at the end of the 19th century. Several of the artists who lived on Tite Street were members of the New English Arts Club, a group formed to protest the extreme conservatism of the Royal Academy. The American artist James McNeill Whistler had his controversial White House (1878; since replaced) designed for him by E.W. Godwin, one of the leading architects of the day. Godwin also designed the Tower House at No. 44 (now modified) and the interior of No. 34 for Oscar Wilde. Wilde lived here from his marriage in 1884 to his arrest in 1895. Augustus John's studio was at No. 33 and society portrait painter John Singer Sargent lived at No. 31.

▶ **STARTS**

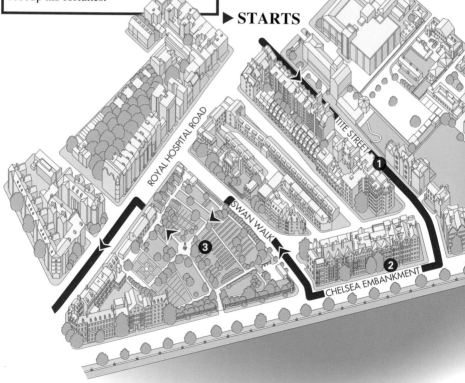

❷ Ignoring the creative fomentation in Tite Street, local planners insisted on a conventional look for the fine houses built in the 1870s along the brand new **Chelsea Embankment.** Richard Norman Shaw built Nos 18, 17, 15, 11, 10, 9 and 8 in his trademark 'Queen Anne Style' and E.W. Godwin was forced to forget his desire for fashionable simplicity when he built Nos 6, 5 and 4. Conventional or not, the houses were always sought after and in the 20th century, Mick Jagger, Paul Getty II and Gerald Scarfe were among the celebrity residents who passed through.

*Lavender Walk at the public entrance to Chelsea Physic Gardens*

The new Embankment (1871) was part of an unromantic but much needed scheme to improve drains and sewage, clear slums and ease traffic. Carlyle, who lived in Cheyne Row, approved of the measures – though others, including Whistler's boatman, mourned the passing of old Chelsea, with its waterfront of coopers, potteries, boatyards and alehouses.

❸ A right turn onto Swan Walk brings you to the **Chelsea Physic Garden** (1673), an idyllic spot in summer and a reminder of the days when the village of Chelsea was surrounded by orchards and farms. The botanic garden – London's first – was expanded by physician Sir Hans Sloane in 1712, and is packed with medicinal plants from around the world. A guided trail takes you past some of the most intriguing species: among them, yams from Mexico (the original plant source of the contraceptive pill); meadowsweet, used to make aspirin; and the bog bean *Menyanthes trifoliata,* harvested as a cure for rheumatism. (Note the restricted opening times: Apr-Oct, Wed noon-5pm; Sun 2-6pm.)

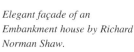

*Lamp at Chelsea Embankment.*

*Elegant façade of an Embankment house by Richard Norman Shaw.*

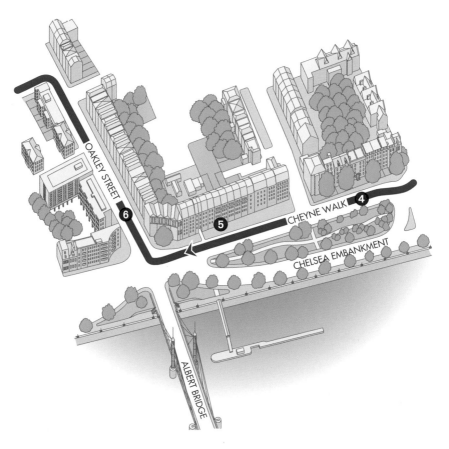

**4 Cheyne Walk,** separated from the Embankment by gardens, attracted more celebrated residents. George Eliot (1819-80) died at No. 4, a few months after her marriage at the age of 61. The poet Algernon Swinburne and artist Dante Gabriel Rossetti shared a house at No.16, keeping an exotic menagerie of animals, including peacocks, whose screeches disturbed the neighbours.

*Memorial to Rossetti (1828-82), poet and painter, in the Chelsea Embankment garden.*

*Above: Albert Bridge (1873), with its tollhouses still standing. Below: bridge detail.*

**5** When Chelsea was surrounded by meadows and market gardens, Sir Thomas More, advisor and friend to Henry VIII, built a country house next to the river. Hans Holbein the younger stayed there before he became Court Painter, and More's wife wrote plaintively to her husband of his 'right fair house' with its garden and orchard while he was imprisoned in the Tower. Henry VIII so liked More's house that he built his own nearby on the site now occupied by **Nos 19-26 Cheyne Walk.** His manor house was demolished in 1753 after the death of its last occupant Sir Hans Sloane (who gave his name to Sloane

Square and whose collection was the basis for today's Natural History Museum). Part of the original garden lies beyond the end wall of Cheyne Mews. From Cheyne Walk there is a view of the pink-and-white **Albert Bridge,** prettiest when lit up at night. The cantilever and suspension bridge was designed in 1873 by R.M. Ordish and its tollhouses still stand.

*Robert Falcon Scott's house on Oakley Street.*

**6** A right turn takes you up **Oakley Street,** past a house (No. 56) once occupied by Antarctic explorer Robert Falcon Scott. Oscar Wilde kept a low profile at his mother's house, No. 87, in an attempt to escape some of the persecution he suffered on account of his homosexuality. In 1895, Wilde was arrested and sentenced to two years in jail with hard labour.

43

**7** Another Chelsea resident who fell foul of the law was essayist and poet Leigh Hunt, who was sent to jail for two years for calling the Prince Regent "a fat Adonis at fifty". He lived at No. 22 Upper Cheyne Row, was a champion of John Keats, and was well respected despite Blackwood's Magazine's jibes against his lowly origins (labelling his work as from the 'Cockney School of Poetry'). Around the corner at 24 Cheyne Row is the Queen Anne house in which the Scottish historian and philosopher Thomas Carlyle lived for 47 years, 40 of them with his wife Jane, one of the most evocative letter-writers in the English language. **Carlyle's House** is open in summer and crammed with personal objects, portraits, furniture and mementoes. (Open Apr-Oct Wed-Fri 2pm-5pm, Sat and Sun 11am-5pm.)

**8** Head right along Lordship Place, past the **Crossed Keys** pub (where you could pause for refreshment), to **Chelsea Old Church.** Henry VIII married Jane Seymour here before their official state wedding; and Thomas More built a private chapel. More was Henry VIII's trusted adviser and friend, but ran into trouble when he refused to accept the King's divorce and the validity of his marriage to Anne Boleyn, or swear the Oath of Supremacy to Henry as head of the Church of England. He was taken to the Tower of London, imprisoned and executed there in 1535.

**9** **Old Church Street** is the oldest thoroughfare in Chelsea, now a side road between the busy Embankment and the shops of the King's Road. Off it is **Justice Walk,** with an old courthouse whose cells were used as wine cellars by merchant H. Allen Smith in the 19th century. Fashionistas shouldn't miss shoe shop **Manolo Blahnik** at 49 Old Church Street.

**10** Justice Walk brings you to **Lawrence Street,** where novelist Tobias Smollett lived at No. 16. This was also home of the Chelsea China factory. Chelsea was a major production centre for pottery in the 18th century, as the river was handy for transport and there was plenty of marshy ground for dumping factory waste. The Huguenot Nicholas Sprimont was inspired by the clear colours and delicate decorative detail of French Sèvres porcelain and was ready to match its quality: as much as 90 per cent of some Chelsea pottery lines was destroyed if the quality wasn't up to scratch. Some fine examples can be seen at the Victoria and Albert Museum.

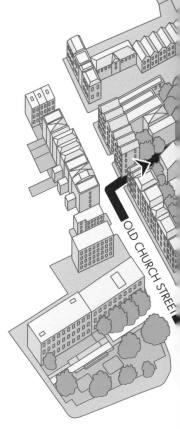

OLD CHURCH STREET

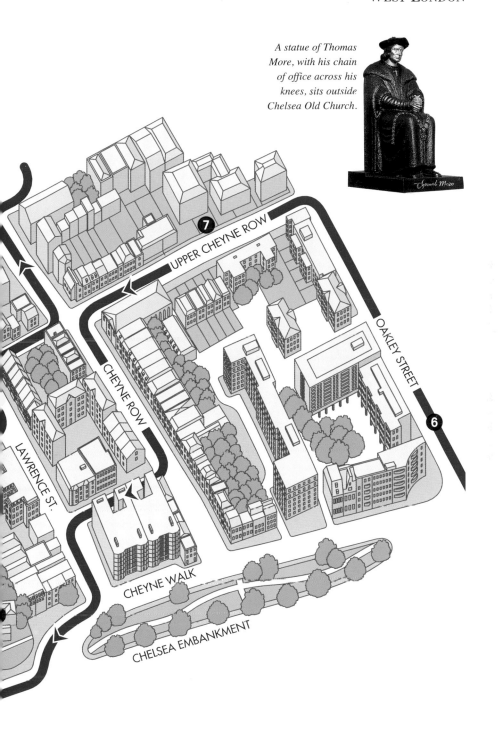

*A statue of Thomas More, with his chain of office across his knees, sits outside Chelsea Old Church.*

Thomas More

# Mayfair

When architect John Nash built Regent Street in the 1800s, he had a kind of social firebreak in mind, keeping apart the artisans and traders of Soho from newly developed Mayfair. The divide still exists. Whereas Soho's fashion and nightlife seems to live by its own law of perpetual motion, Mayfair is the English establishment frozen in aspic. P.G. Wodehouse's Jeeves and Bertie Wooster had their fictional home at Half Moon Street. Afternoon tea at 4pm: take it at Brown's. Hunting shooting and fishing: buy the kit at gunmakers by royal appointment Holland & Holland. As in *Alice Through the Looking Glass*, you may find a walk through Mayfair a curious experience: a mirror that refuses to reflect, its image stays the same while the world around it changes.

*Lawrence Holoscenet's sculpture* Allies *(Churchill and Roosevelt) on Old Bond Street.*

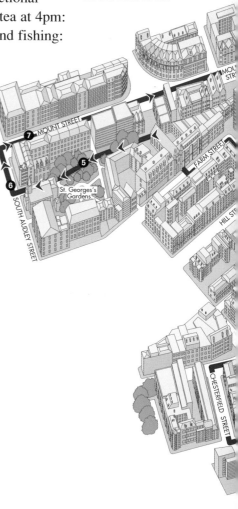

▶ **STARTS**
Half Moon Street. Nearest tube: Green Park. Exit from the tube station entrance on to Piccadilly (north side) and walk left three blocks to Half Moon Street.

■ **ENDS**
Albemarle Street. Nearest tube: Green Park.

*Piccadilly.*

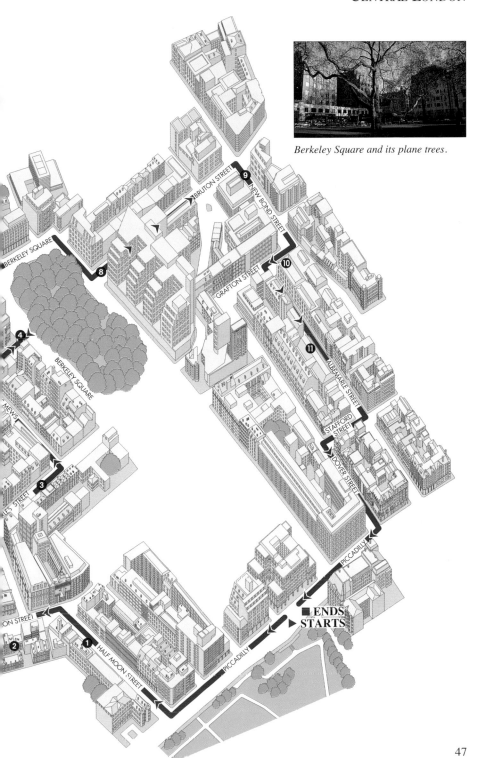

*Berkeley Square and its plane trees.*

BRUTON STREET

NEW BOND STREET

BERKELEY SQUARE

GRAFTON STREET

BERKELEY SQUARE

MEWS

ALBEMARLE STREET

STAFFORD STREET

DOVER STREET

ES STREET

PICCADILLY

ON STREET

■ ENDS
▶ STARTS

HALF MOON STREET

PICCADILLY

# MAYFAIR

**1** Novelist P.G. Wodehouse gave Bertie Wooster and his manservant Jeeves a pied-à-terre on **Half Moon Street,** handy for the gentlemen's clubs of Mayfair and Pall Mall. Wooster would undoubtedly have had his hair cut at G. F. Trumper, which still wafts cologne from 9 Curzon Street.

**2** The area to the south of Curzon Street is known as **Shepherd Market,** scene of riotous fairs held in the first fortnight in May beginning in the late 17th century (from which the district got its name). New residents were offended by the city's 'chiefest nursery of evil' and the fairs were banned in 1764 when the area was redeveloped. Back in Curzon Street, **The Curzon** shows arty films and boasts the comfiest seats of all the capital's cinemas. For the price of an ordinary ticket, you can sit in a box and stave off hunger by bringing your own picnic. A right turn takes you into Chesterfield Street, with its well-preserved façades. Beau Brummell (1778-1840), the original dandy, lived at No. 4.

*South Audley Street.*

*Ornamental statue, Berkeley Square.*

**3** Another right turn into Charles Street brings you to **The Running Footman** pub on the corner of Hay's Mews. The pub is on the circuit of a sedan chair race which takes place every May. The chair carriers of the 18th century were supposed to keep to the middle of the street, but, in an early version of road rage, would lose no opportunity to ram pedestrians with their poles.

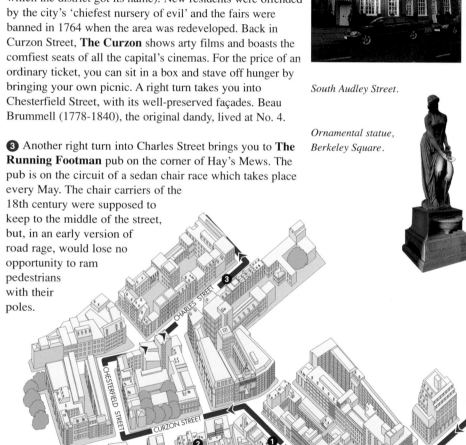

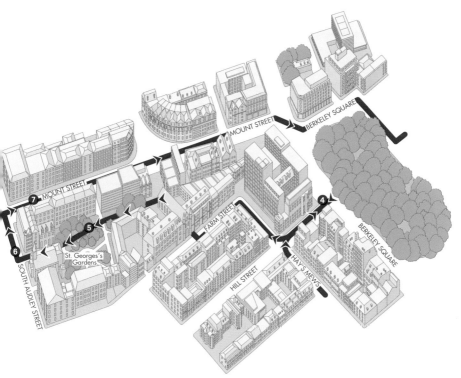

**4** At Hill Street, cut through to **Berkeley Square**. No. 44 is now the **Clermont** gambling club. You can catch a glimpse of the interior, designed for Lady Isabella Finch in 1742-4 by William Kent and one of the grandest of London's 18thC houses. The long-running club **Annabel's** is in the basement.

**5** There are no nightingales to be heard singing in Berkeley Square (too much traffic). But you may see goldcrests feeding in the early morning or hear a song thrush in **St George's Gardens,** a secret and wonderful oasis of plane trees and palms off Farm Street. Next to them is the Jesuit **Church of the Immaculate Conception** with a fine altarpiece by Pugin. It's one of the few remaining Catholic churches in London where mass is sung in Latin.

*Fountain, St George's Gardens.*

**6** 'The name's Bond, James Bond' is a phrase which seems made for **South Audley Street.** Spy shops at Nos 59 and 62 advertise themselves as purveyors of fine bugs, infra-red cameras and all manner of snooping devices.

**7** **Mount Street** is where ladies-who-lunch come to have their roots retouched at the handful of celebrity hairdressers. The long row of specialist shops include best-quality meat and game at **Allens,** the butcher at No. 117; and Havana cigars at **Sautter's,** No. 106. Here too are cutters, humidor accessories, signed photographs of happy customers and some fine ashtrays – including one emblazoned with a huge fat cigar and the words 'Gentlemen You May'.

**8** The route now takes you back into Berkeley Square. One early morning in 1813, Beau Brummell was walking home with a friend when he spotted a crooked sixpence in the gutter. Claiming that it would bring him better luck at the gaming tables, he drilled a hole in it and fastened it to his watch chain before going to bed. He then went on to have an amazing improvement in fortune – or so Mayfair gambling lore says. Gambling was a national obsession in the 18th and 19th centuries, and entire fortunes were lost in a single night in clubs such as **Whites,** No. 37 St James's Street.

Leave Berkeley Square by **Bruton Street,** home to several galleries dealing in heavyweight international artists. On the opposite side of the road is the acclaimed restaurant, **The Square.** If you decide on lunch there, be sure to reserve in advance (020 7495 7100).

*Bond Street: if you have to ask the price, you can't afford it.*

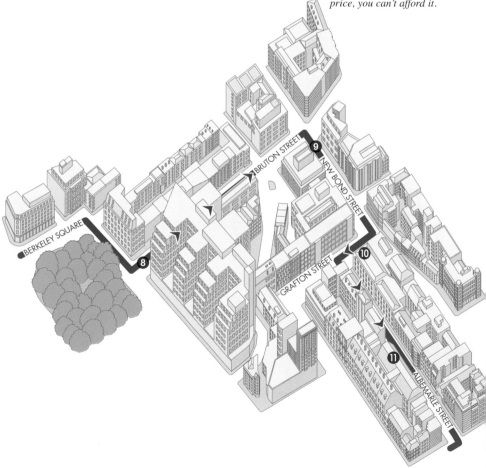

**9** Turn right into **New Bond Street:** Hermès, Max Mara, Donna Karan and Nicole Farhi all rub shoulders in this short stretch. The café in the **Nicole Farhi** basement is good for brunch, coffee or a cocktail. At this point, take another right turn into Albemarle Street.

*Arcade between Albemarle Street and Bond Street.*

**10** A tiny museum at the **Royal Institution,** No. 21, includes a recreation of the lab where Michael Faraday discovered the laws of electromagnetics in the 1830s. The Faraday lectures are still given here every year. Back at the turn of the 18th century, the lectures here were as voguish as the labels on Bond Street, with (female) fans of the charismatic chemistry professor Humphry Davy as keen to attend his lectures as fashionistas are to fight their way into a catwalk show today. The **Faraday Museum** is open Mon-Fri 9am-5pm.

**11** Further down Albemarle Street at No. 30 is **Brown's Hotel,** where Rudyard Kipling finished *The Jungle Book* when he was a guest here in 1894. Come here for an Imperial-style high tea with all the trimmings, including butler service. (Tea is served Mon-Sun 3-6pm throughout the year, reservations are required. Tel. 020 7493 6020.) However, you'll probably have more fun at **Automat,** Carlos Amada's American brasserie at 33 Dover Street (Tel. 020 7499 3033). One section of the restaurant is laid out like the dining car of an old train, and the place offers first-class, diner classics such as hefty burgers, light cheesecake and fresh clam chowder.

*Left: Brown's Hotel, where tea (above) is an English institution.*

# St James's and Piccadilly

■ **ENDS**
PICCADILLY
CIRCUS

REGENT STREET

PICCADILLY

JERMYN STREET

REGENT STREET

DUKE OF YORK STREET

CHARLES II STREET

ST JAMES'S SQUARE

ST JAMES'S SQUARE

KING STREET

PALL MALL

ST JAMES'S STREET

MALBOROUGH ROAD

▶ **STARTS**
Admiralty Arch
Nearest tube: Charing
Cross.
Exit from the tube at
Trafalgar Square. Cross
the square to Admiralty
Arch and the Mall.

I n the early 19th century, the great architect, John Nash, conceived an ambitious scheme to link his Regent's Park to the north with Carlton

*Waterloo Place.*

House to the south, which was then home of his patron, the Prince Regent. This walk begins at the start of Nash's route, diverges into the gentlemanly district of St James's, then returns to Nash at Piccadilly Circus. From here, Nash's route marches on towards the park via grand, sweeping Regent Street and Oxford Circus.

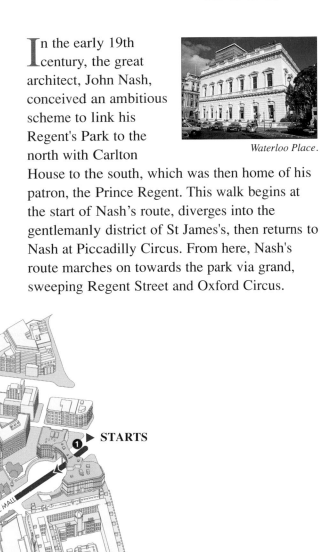

▶ **STARTS**

THE MALL

HAYMARKET

WATERLOO PLACE

■ **ENDS**
Piccadilly Circus.
Nearest tube: Piccadilly
Circus.

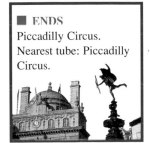

*The Institute of Contemporary Arts in Carlton House Terrace.*

**1** The view through **Admiralty Arch** down The Mall to Buckingham Palace is splendid. Until they were built by Sir Aston Webb in 1911, the capital had no processional route for its royal family.

**2** Walking up the north side of The Mall, you pass **The Mall Galleries** (open daily), showing exhibitions of conventional contemporary art. At the bottom of the Duke of York Steps, the lively **Institute of Contemporary Arts** presents film, theater and discussion, with a bookshop and café (open Tues-Sun, noon-late). Stretching along either side of the steps, pristine **Carlton House Terrace** presents its splendid rear to The Mall. Replacing Carlton House, it was Nash's last work, resplendent (of course) in Doric columns and gleaming stucco.

*Monument to the Crimean War in Waterloo Place.*

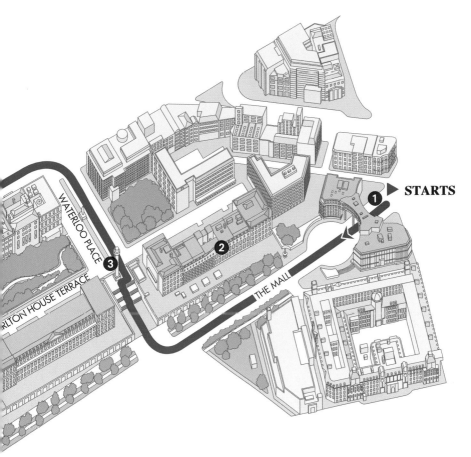

❸ The splendour of **Carlton House Terrace's** layout is capped by the **Duke of York's Column,** designed by Benjamin Wyatt (1831-4), and approached by a broad flight of steps from The Mall. The Duke of York in question (statue by Sir Richard Westmacott) was the second son of George III and is best known today for the nursery rhyme about him and his ten thousand men.

❹ **Pall Mall** is where the French game of *pelle malle* was played with mallet and ball. When it became a fashionable boulevard, the name stuck. It is known for its gentlemen's clubs, whose splendid 19thC façades predominate. Along the stretch leading up to Waterloo Place are the **Reform Club** (No. 104; classically clubby interior around an inner courtyard); the **Travellers' Club** (No. 106; lovely façade by Sir Charles Barry); and Decimus Burton's stunning **Athenaeum.** Its pair, across Waterloo Place, is by Nash, remodelled by Burton, but it lacks the purity of the Athenaeum.

*Monument to Wellington in Waterloo Place.*

**⑤ St James's Palace** was built by Henry VIII on a human scale around four courts. The Gatehouse is the most striking Tudor survivor here, but the Chapel Royal, which continues its tradition of fine choral music, also dates from that time. Opposite the Palace, in Marlborough Road, is the **Queen's Chapel** (Inigo Jones, 1627), the first English church in the classical style.

*Guardsman outside St James's Palace.*

**⑥** Shops which have for generations provided gentlemen with the necessities of life proliferate in **St James's Street.** Here are venerable cigar merchants, wine merchants, gunsmiths, hatters, pharmacies. **Lock & Co** (No. 6) and **Berry Brothers and Rudd** (No. 3) are both very old, with beautiful panelled interiors. On the uneven floor of Berry Brothers stand great scales, first used for weighing tea and coffee, but since 1765, for weighing illustrious members of society: the dandy Beau Brummel, the poet Lord Byron and John Nash himself were all regular weight-watchers. A shelf of ledgers record the results, with excuses: 'after an ample dinner', and 'with large hat'. An arch beside the shop leads to **Pickering Place,** the smallest square in London. If its cocktail time, walk on to **Dukes Hotel** (off map), tucked away off St James's Place, where the best dry Martini in town is served with suitable flourish.

*Outside the cigar shop in St James's Street.*

*The venerable wine merchant, Berry Brothers and Rudd Ltd.*

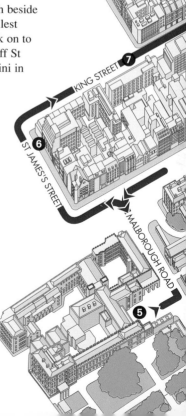

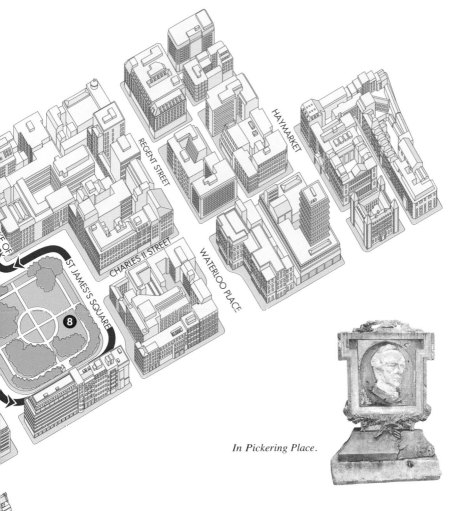

*In Pickering Place.*

*Corner of St James's Square.*

**7** Art dealers abound in and around **King Street,** which is home to one of the world's great auction houses, **Christie's.**

**8** **St James's Square** was developed by the Earl of St Albans in the mid-17th century and has been a stomping ground of the upper crust ever since. As you cross Charles II Street, look down to the **Theatre Royal, Haymarket,** which has the unmistakable stamp of its architect, Nash.

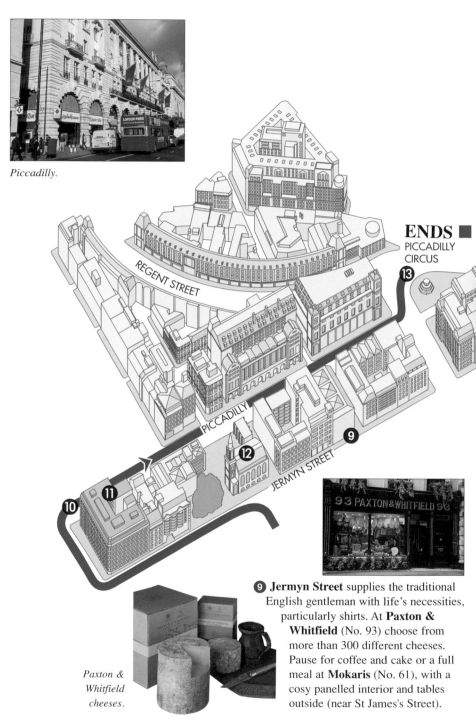

Piccadilly.

**ENDS** ■
PICCADILLY
CIRCUS

REGENT STREET

PICCADILLY

JERMYN STREET

9 3 PAXTON & WHITFIELD 9

Paxton &
Whitfield
cheeses.

**9** **Jermyn Street** supplies the traditional English gentleman with life's necessities, particularly shirts. At **Paxton & Whitfield** (No. 93) choose from more than 300 different cheeses. Pause for coffee and cake or a full meal at **Mokaris** (No. 61), with a cosy panelled interior and tables outside (near St James's Street).

*Above: Plaque on St James's Church.*

*Right: Fortnum & Mason.*

**❿ Piccadilly.** The origin of the name lies with Robert Baker, a 17thC tailor who, with money he made from selling stiff collars called 'picadils', built a house derisively known as 'Piccadilly Hall'.

**⓫ Fortnum & Mason** is a luxury grocery store where assistants in tailcoats will sell you anything from *foie gras* to *marrons glacés*. Almost next door is **Hatchards,** the bookshop, and towards Piccadilly Circus, **Waterstones.** Books now occupy all five floors of this 1930s building, with armchairs, sofas and lots of book signings. There is a great view from the fifth-floor café, a good place for lunch.

*Angel of Christian Charity, Piccadilly Circus.*

**⓬** Inside Sir Christopher Wren's simple brick church, **St James's,** there is a large galleried room with a decorated vaulted ceiling. The church has a reputation for supporting liberal causes, and has often hosted high-profile memorial services. A lively craft market takes place in the courtyard (Wed-Sat).

*Statue in garden outside St James's.*

**⓭** That perennially favourite meeting place, **Piccadilly Circus,** lacks all the grandeur that John Nash envisaged for it, though its tawdry image has been smartened up of late. London's most famous statue is not in fact of **Eros,** God of Love, but the Angel of Christian Charity, a memorial to philanthropist Lord Shaftesbury.

# West End

*Bust of John Nash outside All Souls in Regent Street.*

When their leases reverted to the Crown in 1811, 700 shops and small houses were razed to make way for a Regency superhighway. Regent Street, as it was named, stretches from Pall Mall to Portland Place, and is the masterplan of the playboy Prince Regent (who went on to become George IV). His architect, John Nash, was himself involved in renting out the grand façades of his plan to shops and businesses. The original plan was ambitious – among its features, Regent Street was to culminate in a village of stately homes around Regent's Park, though this never fully materialized. Commerce was always part of the grand design and is still the driving force of the area. The landmark stores on this walk offer everything from fashion to fine art. Among many other fine historic buildings, the Royal Academy of Arts is en route. This walk links up with one that explores St James's and Piccadilly (see pages 52-59).

► **STARTS**
Piccadilly Circus. Nearest tube: Piccadilly Circus. Take the exit for Regent Street (north/east) and walk up Regent Street to the Café Royal.

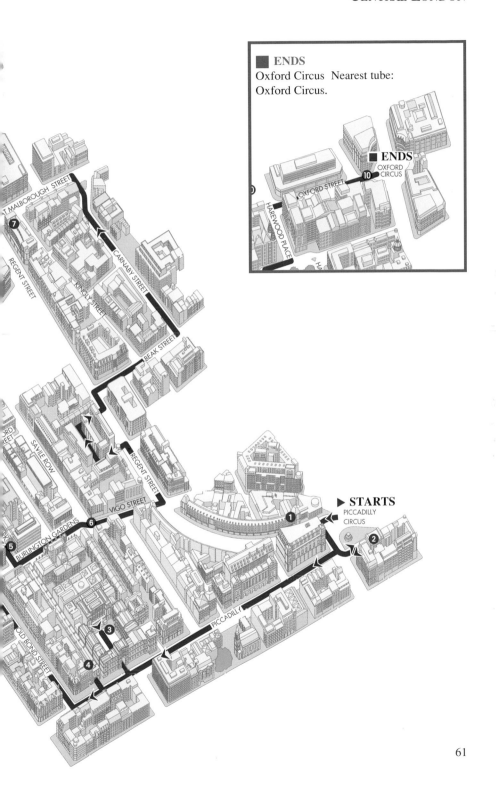

ENDS
Oxford Circus   Nearest tube:
Oxford Circus.

ENDS
OXFORD
CIRCUS

OXFORD STREET

HAREWOOD PLACE

REGENT STREET

GREAT MALBOROUGH STREET

CARNABY STREET

KINGLY STREET

BEAK STREET

SAVILE ROW

REGENT STREET

VIGO STREET

BURLINGTON GARDENS

OLD BOND STREET

STARTS
PICCADILLY
CIRCUS

PICCADILLY

**1** The **Quadrant,** the sweeping curve that leads away from Piccadilly Circus, is virtually all that remains of John Nash's Regent Street. His iron colonnades were demolished in 1846 and replaced by buildings designed by Reginald Blomfield in the 1920s. Two important features of Nash's design have survived: the 'Circuses' where Regent Street meets Piccadilly and Oxford Street. These were designed by Nash to avoid the impression that Regent Street simply crosses these thoroughfares.

Glitzy restaurants have been a feature of the West End since the end of the 19th century. The **Café Royal** on the Quadrant was a bohemian brasserie-style restaurant frequented by Oscar Wilde and the artists Beardsley and Whistler (who signed his bills with the same butterfly motif he used on his paintings).

**2** Another of the top restaurants of the time was the mosaic-studded **Criterion Brasserie** on the opposite side of Piccadilly Circus, which boasted proudly that it could serve 2,000 diners at one sitting. Service is similarly business-like today. Modern counterparts are not far away: the fashionable **Titanic** sits over the Atlantic Bar and Grill at 20 Glasshouse Street (Tel. 0871 332 4219), and the **Oak Room** in the Meridien Hotel at 21 Piccadilly (Tel. 020 7734 8000), is all baroque grandeur and Murano glass chandeliers.

*Criterion Brasserie, Piccadilly Circus.*

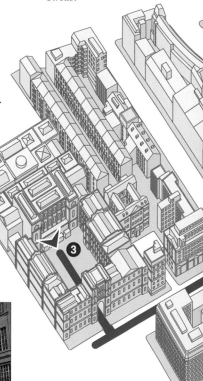

*Nash's Quadrant survived redevelopment.*

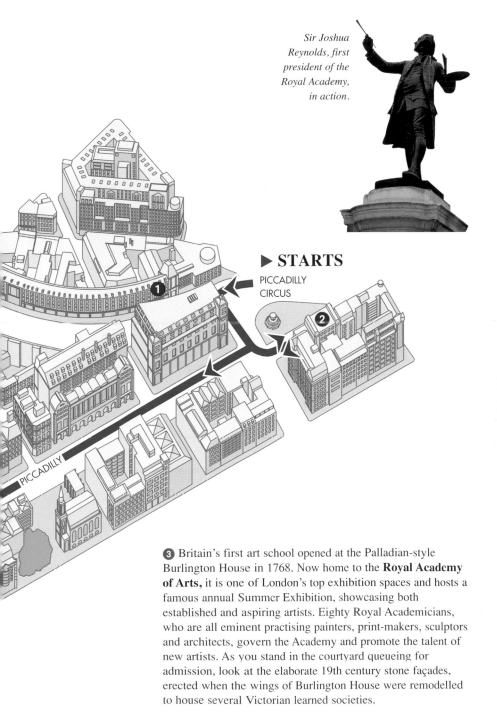

*Sir Joshua Reynolds, first president of the Royal Academy, in action.*

► **STARTS**

**1** PICCADILLY CIRCUS

**2**

PICCADILLY

**3** Britain's first art school opened at the Palladian-style Burlington House in 1768. Now home to the **Royal Academy of Arts,** it is one of London's top exhibition spaces and hosts a famous annual Summer Exhibition, showcasing both established and aspiring artists. Eighty Royal Academicians, who are all eminent practising painters, print-makers, sculptors and architects, govern the Academy and promote the talent of new artists. As you stand in the courtyard queueing for admission, look at the elaborate 19th century stone façades, erected when the wings of Burlington House were remodelled to house several Victorian learned societies.

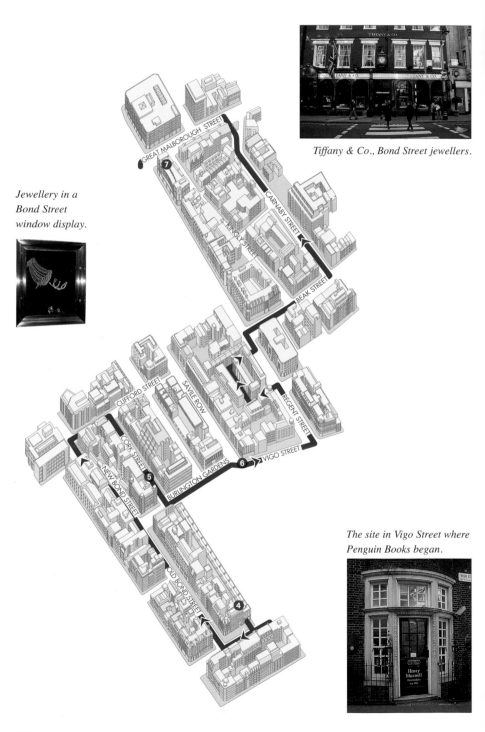

*Tiffany & Co., Bond Street jewellers.*

*Jewellery in a Bond Street window display.*

*The site in Vigo Street where Penguin Books began.*

**4** In the early 1800s, Lord George Cavendish employed Samuel Ware to build **Burlington Arcade,** a classy 'covered lane' of shops, next door to his residence in Burlington House. Cavendish's enemies accused him of building the arcade simply to stop people throwing rubbish into his garden, but Cavendish maintained that the arcade was for the public good and that 'industrious females' would find work in the shops. Later that century, however, when prostitution in London reached epidemic proportions, the arcade became known as a venue for courtesans and their clients. Today it is occupied by exclusive shops selling a variety of luxuries from cashmere sweaters to Irish linen sheets. The rules of the arcade, which include no running, singing, open umbrellas or bicycles, are enforced by costumed officials called beadles, a hangover from the days of Lord Cavendish.

*Burlington Arcade detail.*

**5** You can look but you can't touch the artworks at the Royal Academy, but that's not the case at the commercial galleries in this area. **Agnew's** at 43 Old Bond Street, is one of the city's oldest art dealers (established in 1817) selling 'paintings, drawings and prints of all schools.' The galleries of **Cork Street** made their name in the 1960s. Small shops nearby sell antiques and covetable *objets d'art,* such as the ancient Chinese perfume bottles at **Robert Hall** in Clifford Street.

**6** The route takes you past the bottom of **Savile Row,** *the* place for a sober made-to-measure suit, the last bastion of convention. The spirit of the dandy is alive and well at **Ozwald Boateng,** couture suitmaker with a difference at 9 Vigo Street. Cut around the corner into Heddon Street for Moroccan food and style at **Momo** (No. 27; Tel. 020 7434 4040), for an authentic *tajine* and mint tea. Next door is Momo's sister, a bazaar and tearoom called **Mô** (No. 23; Tel. 020 7734 3999). At No. 21, the **Zinc Bar** (Tel. 020 7434 4040), is a hidden outpost of the Conran restaurant chain – on a human scale and with a short reliable menu and wine list.

**7** Cross Regent Street and walk up **Carnaby Street,** famous for street fashion in the 1960s, now a touristy shopping precinct. At the top you'll find **Liberty,** a department store set up to import oriental goods and famous for its printed fabrics. Despite its Tudor appearance, Liberty was built between the wars, like its neighbour **Dickins and Jones,** when most of Nash's original buildings were pulled down and large stores were put up in their place.

*Liberty department store, its creaky interior an enjoyable place to shop.*

# WEST END

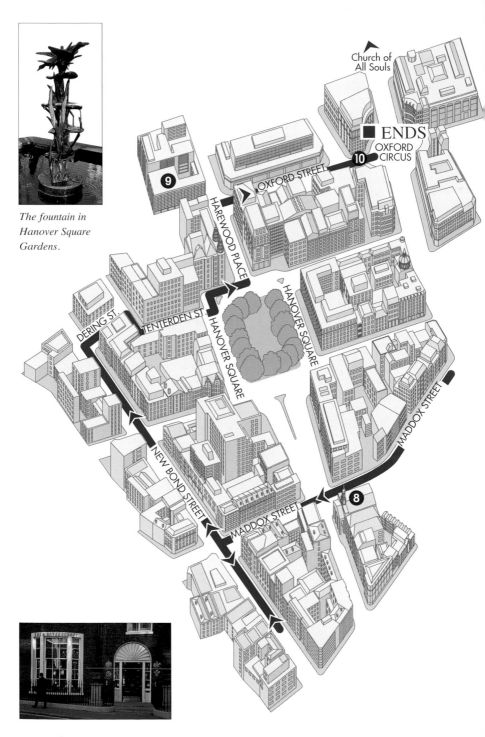

*The fountain in Hanover Square Gardens.*

Church of All Souls

■ ENDS
OXFORD CIRCUS

⑩

⑨

OXFORD STREET

HAREWOOD PLACE

HANOVER SQUARE

TENTERDEN ST.

DERING ST.

HANOVER SQUARE

MADDOX STREET

NEW BOND STREET

MADDOX STREET

⑧

**8** Cross back over Regent Street and head off down Maddox Street until you reach **St George's Church** in **Hanover Square** – the first porticoed church in London. Despite its grimy façade, this church is much favoured by society brides and grooms for tying the knot. In 1886, Theodore Roosevelt walked here to his wedding from Brown's Hotel (see page 51), and Marconi married Beatrice O'Brien here too. Continue along the route to New Bond Street, built around the same time as Oxford Street (1720) and named after Thomas Bond, moneylender to Charles II. Tucked away at No. 34 is **Sotheby's** the auctioneers, recommended for fine-art window shopping and breakfast, lunch or tea in its café (lunchtime booking essential; Tel. 020 7293 5077).

**9** Weave your way back to Hanover Square via Dering Street and the **Rasa** restaurant (No. 6, Tel. 020 7629 1346), which specializes in

vegetarian food from Kerala in southern India. As you head north out of the square on to Oxford Street, notice, on the side of the John Lewis department store straight ahead of you, a characteristic work by **Barbara Hepworth** (1903-75), one of Britain's first abstract sculptors.

*Barbara Hepworth sculpture on the side of John Lewis, Oxford Street.*

**10** **Oxford Street** is Britain's busiest high street, elbowing its way to fame in the 1700s, when local shops hit on the idea of offering indefinite credit. **Oxford Circus** is always packed with shoppers, especially at Christmas. When the Prince of Monaco came here in 1850 he was so dazzled by the lights that he thought the people of England had arranged a special celebration to welcome him. At Oxford Circus the needle spire of Nash's **All Soul's Church** on Langham Place comes into view. From the entrance, a bust of the architect faces Regent Street and gazes out at what has become of his grand civic scheme.

*St George's Church, Hanover Square.*

# Soho

This walk begins at Piccadilly Circus and heads straight into Soho, threading through the restaurant, bar and café-packed streets which have long been the haunt of refugees, artists and professional drinkers. The streets still exude an atmosphere of energy and sleaze. Historically, Soho has been a haven for exiles and outsiders; now it is media territory, and a significant place on the gay London map. The walk continues through the heart of London's Chinatown and ends in Leicester Square.

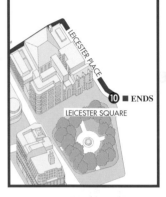

■ **ENDS**
Leicester Square.
Nearest tube: Leicester Square.

▶ **STARTS**
Piccadilly Circus. Nearest tube: Piccadilly Circus. Exit from the tube at Shaftesbury Avenue. Walk for a couple of minutes away from the Circus and take the second left into Great Windmill Street.

*Fresh Chinese vegetables for sale in Gerrard Street.*

❶ You start this walk along **Great Windmill Street,** a shabby looking place headed by the old Windmill Theatre, now a table dancing club. The playhouse was formerly well known for its theatrical tableaux in the Thirties – when the Windmill was the first London theatre where nudity was permitted on stage – but only on condition that the players didn't move.

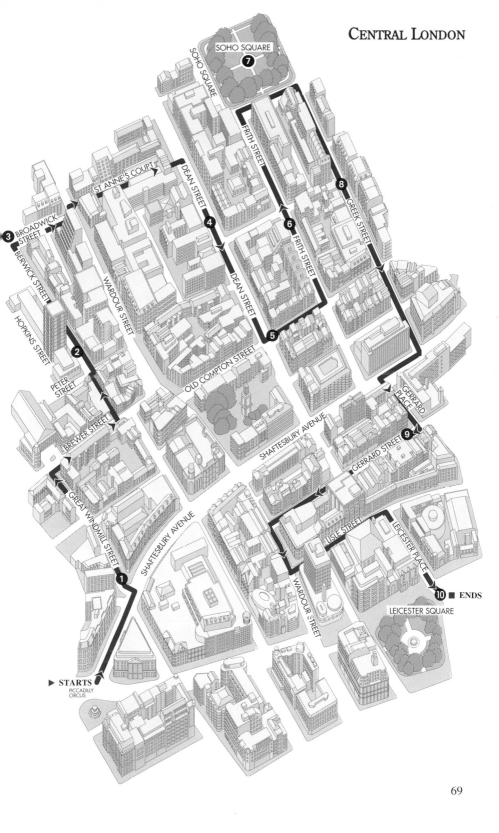

SOHO SQUARE

⑦

SOHO SQUARE

FRITH STREET

ST ANNE'S COURT

DEAN STREET

④

⑧

GREEK STREET

⑥

BROADWICK STREET

❸

FRITH STREET

BERWICK STREET

DEAN STREET

HOPKINS STREET

②

⑤

OLD COMPTON STREET

PETER STREET

WARDOUR STREET

GERRARD PLACE

BREWER STREET

SHAFTESBURY AVENUE

⑨

GERRARD STREET

GREAT WINDMILL STREET

LISLE STREET

LEICESTER PLACE

SHAFTESBURY AVENUE

①

WARDOUR STREET

⑩ ■ ENDS

LEICESTER SQUARE

▶ STARTS
PICCADILLY
CIRCUS

**2** Take the alleyway beside **Lina Stores,** a treasure trove of Italian delicacies, including pasta in all shapes and sizes, to **Berwick Street market** (daily except Sunday), where barrows of cheap fruit and veg still just outnumber stalls selling olives, herbs and homemade breads. The market developed from the 18thC shopkeepers' habit of displaying wares on the pavement outside their shops, but the market was not officially recognized until 1892. Today the stalls are backed by sari and silk shops, the smell of fast food frying and the sound of rare tracks spilling from nearby record and CD outlets.

*Berwick Street market.*

**3** At the top of Berwick Street, **Broadwick Street** was the scene of a cholera outbreak in 1854. A local doctor, John Snow, suspected that its cause was polluted water, and had the street water pump sealed off. The only locals who survived the epidemic were those who avoided water and stuck to beer. His discovery led to a breakthrough in the study of the disease and he is commemorated by a handleless pump – and the name of a pub nearby.

*Floridita, a cocktail and Cuban music bar.*

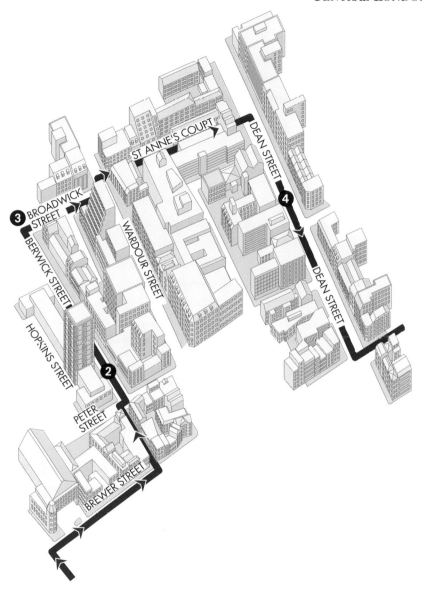

④ Cross Wardour Street, home to movie distributors and the Conran Spanish restaurants **Meza** and **Floridita,** and take the cut-through called St Anne's Court into **Dean Street.** Huguenots (French Protestants fleeing Louis XIV's France) made their base in Dean Street and later the pub at No. 49 (with restaurant above called the **French House**) was the unofficial HQ of the Free French during World War II. It serves beer by the half (no pints), wine and spirits and was a hangout of artists and writers in the Fifties. So too is the members-only **Colony Club** at No. 41, which has been patronized by Francis Bacon and the current crop of Brit artists. London's arts establishment also gathers at the **Groucho Club** at No. 44, at **Blacks,** and at **Soho House** on Greek Street.

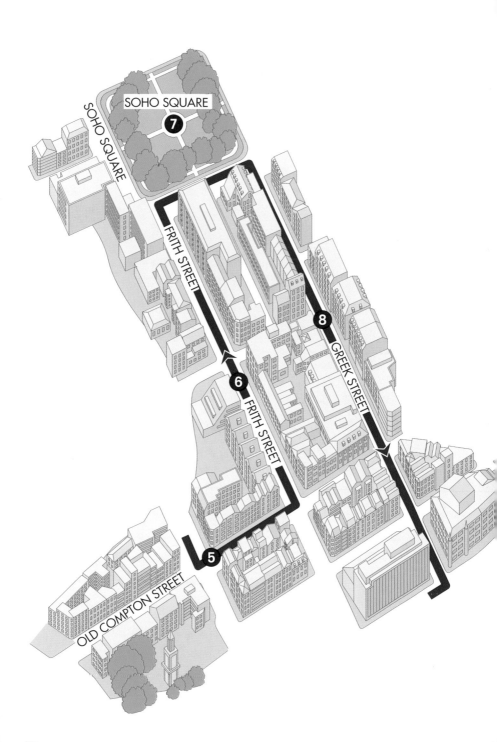

SOHO SQUARE

7

SOHO SQUARE

FRITH STREET

8

GREEK STREET

6

FRITH STREET

5

OLD COMPTON STREET

*Above, the former home away from home of archetypal roué, Jeffrey Barnard.*

**5 Old Compton Street** crosses Dean Street and is the epicentre of London's extrovert gay scene, with cafés such as Balans (open 24 hours, every day except 25th December). The street is also known for specialist liquor off-licences: Gerry's is at No 74; Camisa the Italian deli is at No. 61, tiny but crammed with wonderful things to eat; and the old-fashioned Patisserie Valerie is at No 44, a congenial stopping place for an Anglo-French combination of a croissant and a pot of tea.

**6** Turn up **Frith Street,** stopping at **Bar Italia,** No. 22, for a quick shot of caffeine and pure drama in the form of either Italian opera or football on the huge wide-screen TV. Appropriately, J Logie Baird demonstrated the first moving images on a prototype television on these premises in 1926. Across the road at No 47 is **Ronnie Scott's,** centre of the Soho jazz scene in the 1950s and still attracting some jazz greats – if you're on a tight budget, do all your drinking before you get to the club.

**7** At the top of Frith Street is **Soho Square.** On summer weekdays this park is surrounded by bike messengers stretched out on their bikes waiting for the next call, and crammed full of office workers sitting on the grass eating their lunch. It's the only patch of green around. On the corner is the **House of St Barnabas** (1746), the sole survivor from Soho's aristocratic past, with a beautiful rococo interior (call to arrange a tour, Tel. 0207 437 1894). The house is now a centre offering training and advice to homeless people.

**8** Skirt the southern edge of the square and head back down **Greek Street,** named after Greek Christians fleeing Ottoman persecution in the 17th century. Casanova and Thomas de Quincey once lodged on this street. At No 29 is the **Coach and Horses** pub, long-time watering hole of Soho personality Jeffrey Barnard. When he was too drunk to write his newspaper column, the line 'Jeffrey Barnard is unwell' would appear – a catch phrase that was adopted by Keith Waterhouse as the title for his successful West-End show based on Barnard's life.

*Soho Square*

*Greek Street.*

73

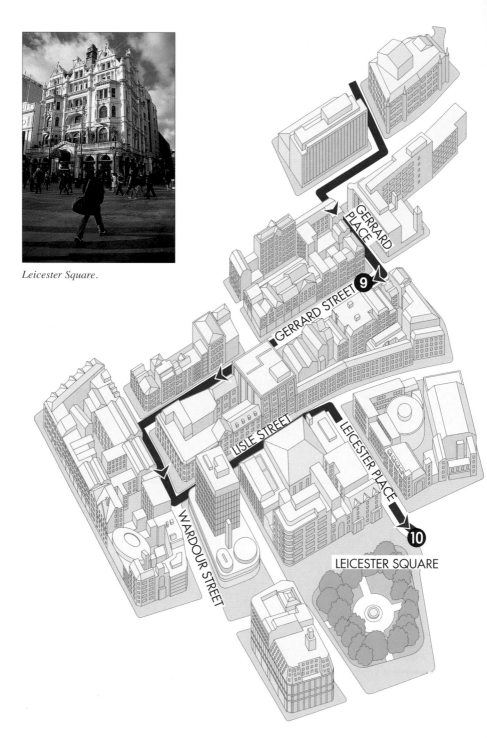

*Leicester Square.*

GERRARD PLACE

GERRARD STREET **9**

LISLE STREET

LEICESTER PLACE

**10**

WARDOUR STREET

LEICESTER SQUARE

*Gerrard Street dragons.*

rose sellers, and crowds flock around buskers and street entertainers. You might find yourself held behind barriers on film premiere nights when the Hollywood stars show up. Long a center of popular entertainment, in the 18th and 19th centuries visitors came here for the gaming houses, theaters and bathhouses and now, as then, the square is busy well into the small hours.

*Street performers are a permanent fixture in Leicester Square and Piccadilly Circus.*

**9** Continue to the end of Greek Street and cross Shaftesbury Avenue into **Gerrard Street** via Gerrard Place. This is the main drag of London's Chinatown, lined with restaurants and specialist food shops such as **New Look Fung** supermarket. Despite the faux-pagoda style phone boxes, this street is a genuine centre for the Chinese community who first came here in the Fifties. At the end of January or beginning of February, the street is filled with exploding firecrackers and dancing dragons to celebrate Chinese New Year. Turn left into Lisle Street for Chinese herbalists and for unpretentious Chinese cafés.

*Formal gardens, Leicester Square.*

**10** A right turn down Leicester Place takes you past the church of **Notre Dame de France** with its 1960 murals painted by Jean Cocteau. Continue past London's cheapest repertory cinema, the **Prince Charles,** and enter the bustle of **Leicester Square.** After dark, the place is heaving. Cinema-goers and tourists rub shoulders with club touts and

# Covent Garden

► STARTS

Garrick Street. Nearest tube: Leicester Square. Take the Cranbourn Street exit from the tube, walk down Cranbourn Street and cross St Martin's Lane.

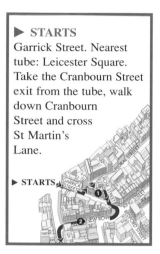

Back in the days of Boswell and Dr Johnson, Covent Garden was known for its coffee houses, dining clubs and theatres such as the Lyceum and the Theatre Royal, run by actor-managers Henry Irving and David Garrick. The city's most famous fruit and vegetable market had its genesis even earlier in the mid-17th century with a few stalls in the fourth Earl of Bedford's back garden. The Cockney dawn chorus of the fruit and veg traders stopped abruptly in 1974, when the market moved to Nine Elms near Vauxhall and Charles Fowler's Central Market building (1831) was converted into an arcade of clothes and souvenir shops, cafés, fast-food outlets and market stalls. Londoners still head to the surrounding streets for entertainment, though they may complain that the area is touristy and commercialized. Covent Garden is both, but it's still worth a visit for the best theatre, opera and restaurants. The most colourful street life in the city can be found here, along a network of shopping streets selling everything from *feng shui* to fashion.

*Salisbury pub.*

❶ As you head down Garrick Street at the start of this walk, you pass the **Garrick Club,** named after the 18thC actor-manager David Garrick. It is one of London's crusty but influential clubs, originally set up to put members of the establishment in contact with writers, performers and artists. It presents a formal face, unlike the rest of the locality. Bars and pubs are at every turn, with one of the oldest and most traditional being the **Lamb and Flag** pub (1623) in Rose Street. This was a dubious location back then, as the writer Dryden was unfortunate enough to discover when he was mugged in the narrow alleyway alongside it.

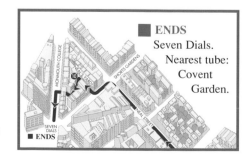

■ ENDS

Seven Dials. Nearest tube: Covent Garden.

76

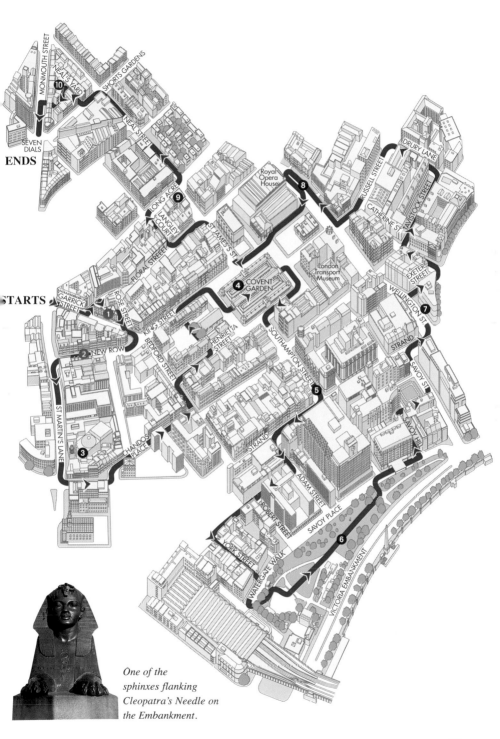

SEVEN DIALS
**ENDS**

MONMOUTH STREET
NEAL'S YARD
SHORTS GARDENS
NEAL STREET

SEVEN DIALS
⑩

SHORTS GARDENS

**STARTS**

GARRICK STREET
ROSE STREET
①
②　NEW ROW
ST MARTIN'S LANE
③
CHANDOS PLACE

LONG ACRE
⑨
LANGLEY COURT
FLORAL STREET
ST JAMES'S ST.
KING STREET
BEDFORD STREET
HENRIETTA STREET
STRAND

Royal Opera House
⑧
RUSSELL STREET
DRURY LANE
CATHERINE ST
TAVISTOCK STREET
EXETER STREET
WELLINGTON ST.
⑦
STRAND

COVENT GARDEN
④

London Transport Museum

SOUTHAMPTON STREET
⑤
SAVOY ST.
SAVOY HILL

ADAM STREET
SAVOY PLACE
⑥
YORK STREET
ROBERT STREET
WATERGATE WALK
VICTORIA EMBANKMENT

*One of the
sphinxes flanking
Cleopatra's Needle on
the Embankment.*

**2** Take a turn to the right, down New Row. When you get to St Martin's Lane, turn left and look out for **Goodwin's Court,** a narrow alleyway of 17thC houses still lit by gaslights, before heading on to Ian Schrager's hotel – **St Martin's Lane** – in a converted cinema. If you are here at lunch or dinner time it's well worth stopping off at its Asia de Cuba restaurant. The Light Bar next to it is, ironically, dark and secluded, and open to hotel guests only at busy times. Skirt your way round gilded molar-shaped stools to get to the brasserie.

*London Transport Museum.*

**3** Pass the domed **Coliseum** – home of the English National Opera – take a left turn

*The globe-topped dome of the Coliseum.*

along Chandos Place, another left into Bedford Street, and then a right into Henrietta Street, from where you can pass through the gateway that leads into the churchyard of **St Paul's** (1633). Known as the 'actor's church' (with memorials to the stars), it was built on the orders of property speculator the 4th Earl of Bedford, who commissioned Inigo Jones to design something that wouldn't involve too much expense. "I would not have it much better than a barn," the Earl is reported to have said. The architect replied that he would give him "the handsomest barn in England," proceeding to erect the hangar-like space.

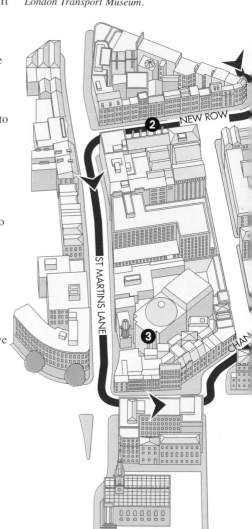

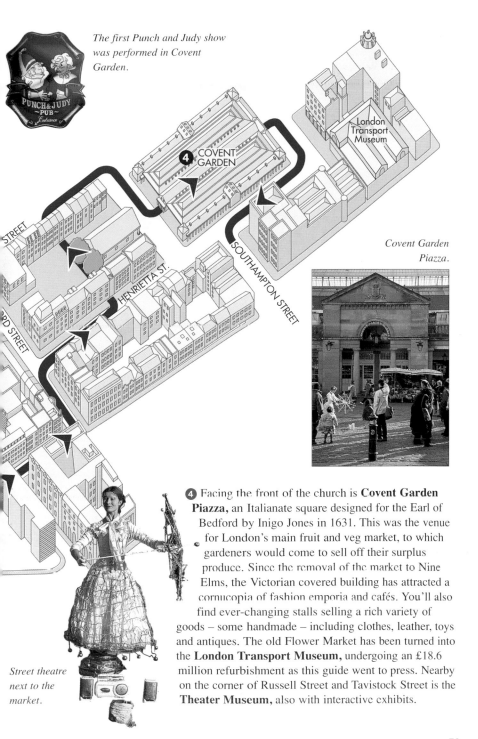

*The first Punch and Judy show was performed in Covent Garden.*

*Covent Garden Piazza.*

*Street theatre next to the market.*

4 Facing the front of the church is **Covent Garden Piazza,** an Italianate square designed for the Earl of Bedford by Inigo Jones in 1631. This was the venue for London's main fruit and veg market, to which gardeners would come to sell off their surplus produce. Since the removal of the market to Nine Elms, the Victorian covered building has attracted a cornucopia of fashion emporia and cafés. You'll also find ever-changing stalls selling a rich variety of goods – some handmade – including clothes, leather, toys and antiques. The old Flower Market has been turned into the **London Transport Museum,** undergoing an £18.6 million refurbishment as this guide went to press. Nearby on the corner of Russell Street and Tavistock Street is the **Theater Museum,** also with interactive exhibits.

**5** Leave the Piazza and the bustle of Covent Garden and follow Southampton Street down to the Strand. Enter into the network of streets named after the Adam brothers, in particular the architect Robert Adam. In the 1770s, the Adam brothers created the **Adelphi,** an imaginative town-within-a-town on the Thames waterfront. The Italianate central terrace was knocked down in 1932 but other parts survive at 1-3 Robert Street, 8 John Adam Street (now the Royal Society of Arts) and 7 Adam Street. From York Street, take Watergate Walk past York Water Gate, a relic from the days when all the private houses along the river had their own – often grand – landing stages.

*York Water Gate.*

**6** Take a stroll through **Victoria Embankment Gardens** for a change of scene, a welcome respite from the hurly-burly. Flanking the gardens is the **Savoy Hotel,** built in 1884-89. It was financed by Richard D'Oyly Carte, managed by César Ritz and had as its first chef the celebrated Auguste Escoffier. Service was a strong point from the start: the hotel recorded guests' likes and dislikes on a card index. D'Oyly Carte also owned the **Savoy Theatre** next door where his Gilbert and Sullivan productions were performed. The following century (and light years away in terms of music), Bob Dylan filmed his famous 'Subterranean Homesick Blues' sequence in an alleyway nearby – flashing up the lyrics on pieces of card before discarding them in as disconsolate a way as the mood of the song.

**7** Plunge back across the Strand to Wellington Street and onward via Exeter Street where, in theme-park vein, signposts inform you that you are now in Theatreland. Back in 1662, the first Punch and Judy show was performed in Covent Garden, followed by the building of dozens of theatres over the years. Among them were the Royal Opera House, the neoclassical **Lyceum** with its stone bas reliefs and fluted columns, and the **Theatre Royal Drury Lane,** with the only surviving Georgian theatre interior in London (and a resident ghost, a Man in Grey). Opposite the main entrance in Catherine Street, the **Nell of Old Drury** pub refers to the story that Nell Gwyn, Charles II's mistress, acted in an earlier theatre on this site in 1665. Around the corner at 36 Tavistock Street, Thomas De Quincey wrote his *Confessions of an English Opium-Eater* in 1821. At 68 Drury Lane, an old-fashioned shop, **Brodie and Middleton,** sells theatrical supplies, clown make-up, false noses and beards.

*Embankment Gardens.*

*Cleopatra's Needle on the Embankment.*

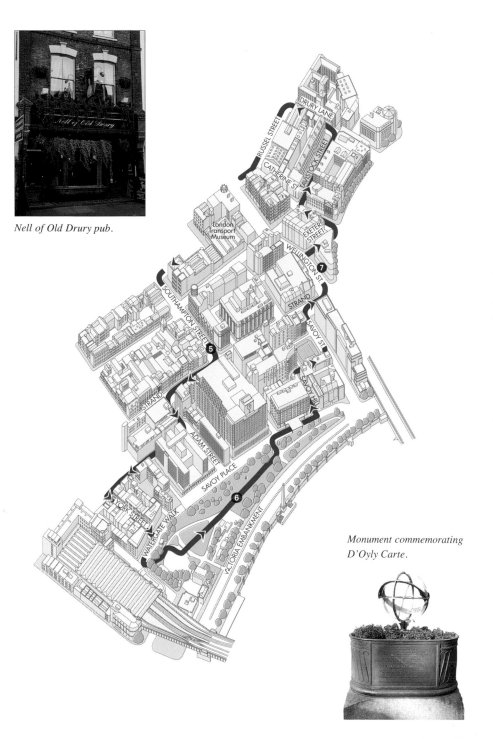

*Nell of Old Drury pub.*

*Monument commemorating D'Oyly Carte.*

**8** Turn right into **Bow Street,** home of the Bow Street runners, a police force set up in 1753 by the lawyer and novelist Henry Fielding in response to the high crime levels of Georgian London. Fielding and his half-brother John presided over the Bow Street Magistrates' Court opposite the Opera House. Known as 'the Blind Beak', John was said to be able to identify 3,000 thieves by voice alone as they appeared before him at the bench. If you want to, peek inside the **Royal Opera House** opposite (revamped at a cost of £214 million) and its glorious iron and glass Floral Hall (open Mon-Sat 10am-3.30pm; at other times to ticket holders only).

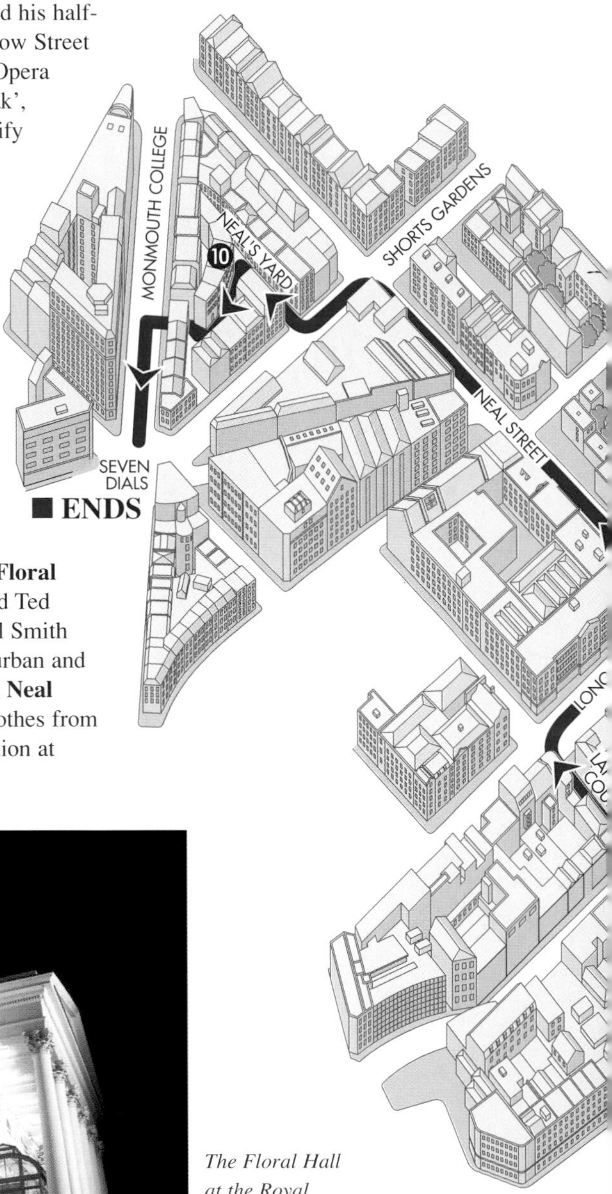

**9** North of the Piazza is shopping nirvana with good hunting grounds for street fashion and designer labels. On **Floral Street** and **Long Acre** you'll find Ted Baker, Diesel Style Lab and Paul Smith shops, and plenty of outlets for urban and teen fashion. Neal Street East on **Neal Street** specializes in gifts and clothes from around the world with more fashion at Shelleys and Press + Bastyan.

MONMOUTH COLLEGE

NEAL'S YARD

SHORTS GARDENS

NEAL STREET

SEVEN DIALS

■ **ENDS**

*The Floral Hall at the Royal Opera House.*

*Bow Street Magistrates' Court.*

🔟 Walk up Neal Street, past the junction with Earlham Street, where the innovative fringe theatre the **Donmar Warehouse** resides. At the junction with Shorts Gardens (look out for the **Kite Store** on the right-hand side), turn left following the signs to **Neal's Yard,** where a dairy, bakery and vegan and vegetarian cafés surround a small courtyard. A walk through either of the narrow passageways off the courtyard (open during business hours) brings you into

*Seven Dials.*

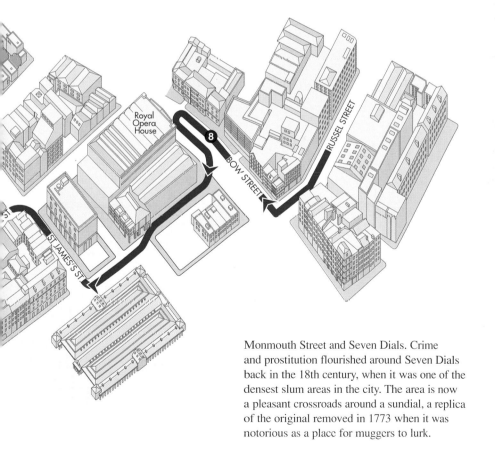

Monmouth Street and Seven Dials. Crime and prostitution flourished around Seven Dials back in the 18th century, when it was one of the densest slum areas in the city. The area is now a pleasant crossroads around a sundial, a replica of the original removed in 1773 when it was notorious as a place for muggers to lurk.

# Aldwych

An inspired redevelopment has turned Somerset House from Admiralty and Inland Revenue offices into an arts venue. The handsome neoclassical courtyard, with its modern 55-jet fountain, is now one of London's finest open-air concert venues in summer. There's ice skating here in midwinter, and Oliver Peyton's Admiralty restaurant and river terrace café serve deft modern British cuisine. Once away from here, the walk has a very different feel, exploring the hidden gardens and passages of the Inns of Court, an area that has been the domain of the legal profession since medieval times. The best time to come here is on a weekday, when the Middle and Inner Temples are open to the public (entrances are locked at weekends and after 9pm), the courts are in session, and the pavements, bookshops and restaurants are buzzing.

▶ **STARTS**
Junction of the Strand and Aldwych. Nearest tube: Embankment. Exit from Embankment tube, walk north up Villiers Street and turn right along the Strand to Somerset House.

■ **ENDS**
Back at starting point. Nearest tube: Embankment.

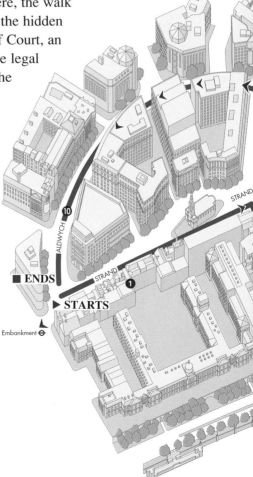

*Middle Temple.*

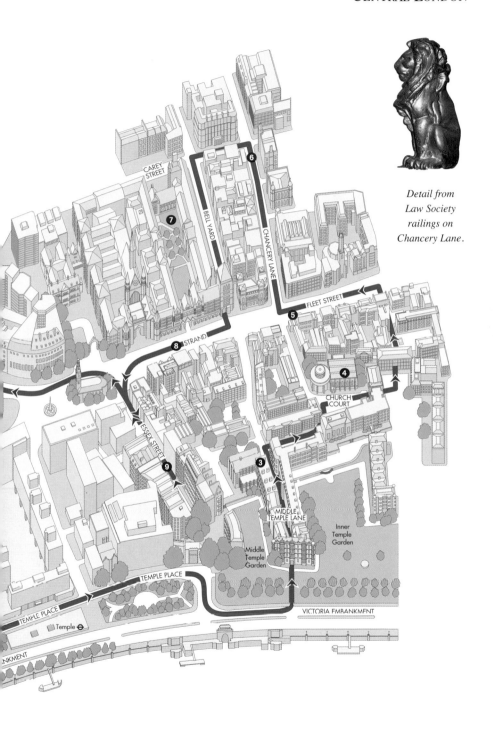

*Detail from
Law Society
railings on
Chancery Lane.*

❶ Britain's finest collection of French Impressionist and Post-Impressionist art can be seen at the **Courtauld Institute Galleries,** named after textiles giant Samuel Courtauld (1865-1947), in Somerset House on the Strand. Among its jewels are paintings by Cézanne, Gauguin, Manet, Monet, Renoir and Van Gogh. (Open Mon-Sat 10am-6pm; Sun and bank hol Mons noon-6pm; admission £5; free admission 10am-2pm every Mon, except bank holidays.)

Overlooking the river, the South Building houses the Gilbert Collection of decorative arts and The Hermitage Rooms which display major exhibitions.

*Silver griffin on Victoria Embankment.*

*View across courtyard from the Courtauld Institute.*

❷ Take time to admire the views of the river from the terrace of Somerset House, then head off to **5 Strand Lane** to see the quirky Roman-style plunge pool restored in the 17th century and fed by a cold spring. Its 19th century proprietor proudly advertised the ten tons of pure spring water which filled the bath daily 'so every bather has the advantage of a continual change of water'. This was at a time when to bathe at home involved a laborious process of filling a hip bath with dozens of jugs of water. In his novel *David Copperfield,* Dickens describes the 'Roman' bath as one in which David had many cold plunges.

The bath is visible through a window from the pathway, but if you want to go inside you must arrange a visit in advance (open May-Sept Wed 1-5pm by appointment only with 24 hours' notice. Tel. 020 7641 5264 or Fax 020 7641 5215).

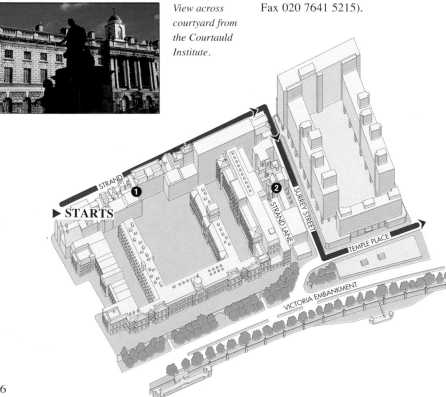

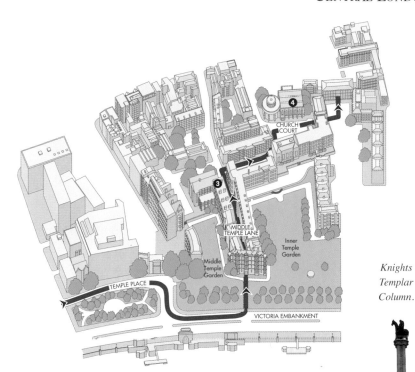

*Knights Templar Column.*

❸ From Temple Place, turn right towards the river and then left along the Embankment. As you walk past the silver griffins, you are officially entering the City of London. Turn left through the entrance to **Middle Temple** and walk up the attractive cobbled lane. The 'Temple' part of the name arose in the 12th century, when the headquarters of the crusading Knights Templar was sited here. The crusaders' cross (a red cross on a white ground) can still be seen, held by a golden lamb, on the façade of Middle Temple Hall. Built in 1573, the hall has an impressive oak double hammerbeam roof and Elizabethan screen. In the 1400s, the Duke of Lancaster and the Duke of York chose as their emblems a red and white rose (respectively) from the Middle Temple gardens. Their subsequent battles for the English crown consequently became known as the Wars of the Roses.

❹ Marble effigies of the Knights Templar can be seen in the circular **Temple Church,** which dates back to the 12th century. Outside the church is another commemoration of the knights: two crusaders share a horse on a statue perched at the top of a column. The

*Temple Place.*

Templars were suppressed in 1312 and their land turned over to the Knights Hospitaller, who then leased it on to lawyers and law students. This area – Inner Temple – is still given over to barristers' chambers, and makes up two of the four Inns of Court – so called because originally barristers not only trained but also lodged and ate there. Trainee barristers must still eat a minimum number of dinners at one of the Inns before they can be called to the Bar.

You'll get a glimpse of the lovely **Inner Temple Gardens** if you deviate south off your route to **Crown Office Row** and look through the magnificent wrought-iron gates, decorated with the Inner Temple pegasus and the Gray's Inn griffin to symbolize the alliance of the two inns.

**5** In a black and white timbered house at 17 Fleet Street, among a jumble of sandwich shops, newspaper stalls and alleyways leading into the Temple area, a narrow stairway takes you to **Prince Henry's Room.** The Prince of Wales feathers and the initials of Henry, son of James I, in the centre of the ceiling give the room its name. The carved wood panelling miraculously survived both the Great Fire in the 17th century, and the Blitz in the 20th; the strapworked plaster ceiling is held together with horsehair and dates from 1610. In the following decades Samuel Pepys wrote his observations on London life and a small exhibition on the celebrated diarist fills the walls. (Open Mon-Fri 11am-2pm).

*Prince Henry's Room.*

**6** The legal bookshops and sober-suited barristers striding around make it clear which profession holds sway in this part of London. **Chancery Lane's** name comes from the fact that Henry III turned over this land to his Lord Chancellor in the 13th century. At **Ede and Ravenscroft,** No. 93, fledgling barristers buy their robes and made-to-measure wigs.

**7** In the **Royal Courts of Justice,** known colloquially as the Law Courts, there are 88 courts in all, and anyone is free to watch a case from the public benches at the back. The pinnacled and turretted courts are seemingly labyrinthine in layout – but are cleverly designed to keep judges apart from counsel, and juries from prosecution and defence. The court complex was designed by G. E. Street, and was hailed as a triumph of Gothic style when completed in 1882. However, the strain of the commission sent him to an early grave. As cameras are not allowed inside the Law Courts, a number of the small shops opposite the main entrance in the Strand will look after your camera – usually in return for a small donation to charity – while you tour the building. Behind lies **Carey Street:** to be 'in Carey Street' was slang for being bankrupt, from the time when bankruptcy courts were located here.

**8** Two surprises lie among the bustle of the Law Courts. First, the **Strand branch of Lloyds Bank,** where tellers sit in front of their screens surrounded by hand-painted Doulton tile panels depicting

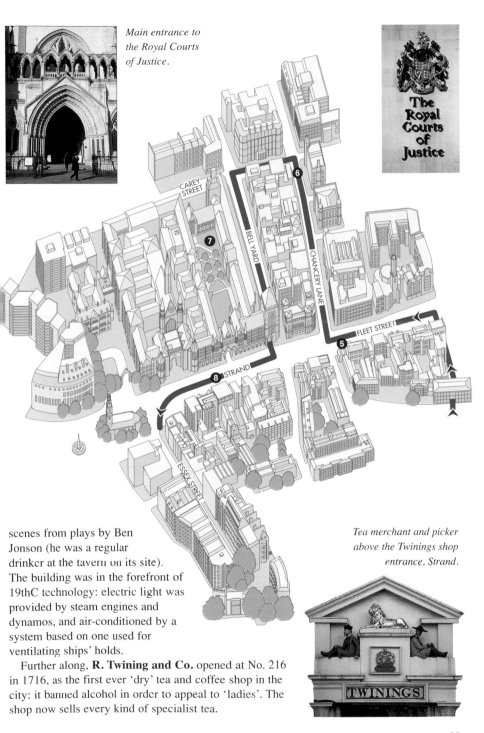

*Main entrance to the Royal Courts of Justice.*

The
Royal
Courts
of
Justice

*Tea merchant and picker above the Twinings shop entrance, Strand.*

scenes from plays by Ben Jonson (he was a regular drinker at the tavern on its site). The building was in the forefront of 19thC technology: electric light was provided by steam engines and dynamos, and air-conditioned by a system based on one used for ventilating ships' holds.

Further along, **R. Twining and Co.** opened at No. 216 in 1716, as the first ever 'dry' tea and coffee shop in the city: it banned alcohol in order to appeal to 'ladies'. The shop now sells every kind of specialist tea.

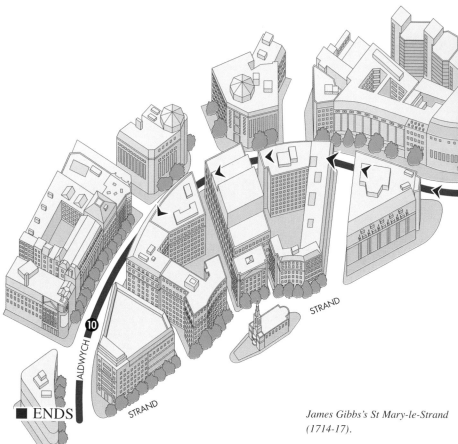

ALDWYCH

10

STRAND

STRAND

■ ENDS

STRAND

Embankment ⊖

*James Gibbs's St Mary-le-Strand (1714-17).*

**9** Nicholas Barbon, a busy speculative builder in Restoration times, pulled down most of **Essex Street** and built a street of 'taverns, alehouses, cookshops and vaulting schools' in its place. Henry Fielding (1707-54), novelist and lawyer, lived on Essex Street, as did many other lawyers of the time. Two pubs worth visiting survive: the Edgar Wallace at No. 40, built on the site of the Essex Head Club founded by Dr Johnson in 1783; and round the corner on Little Essex Street, the Cheshire Cheese, with dark beamy interior and resident ghost.

*One Aldwych.*

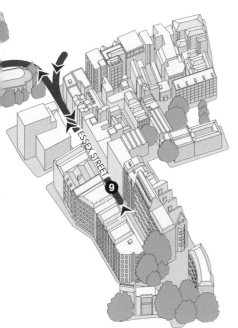

**10** Once the preserve of High Commissions and small theatres, Aldwych is now home to **Bank,** one of the first London restaurants to offer inspired cooking in designer canteen surroundings, and **Woodhams,** a fashionable florist's with a tiny but arty interior. Two contrasting hotels almost rub shoulders here: **One Aldwych** – a hotel doubling as contemporary art gallery, with a superb restaurant named **Indigo;** and the **Waldorf Hilton** (formerly the Waldorf Meridien) — traditional both in style and service, and known for its tea dances.

# Holborn and Two Inns of Court

This is a peaceful walk of hidden parks and gardens, linked by the narrow passageways leading through Gray's Inn and Lincoln's Inn, two of the four Inns of Court. Though they seem like private enclaves, they are open to the public during the week (but closed at weekends) and are a relatively unknown haven in the middle of London's traffic-clogged centre. Ideally, this route should be done at lunchtime, so you can enjoy the beautiful **Lincoln's Inn** (open 12-2.30pm). In summer, take food – there are plenty of places to picnic. Alternatively, if you walk the first Tuesday of the month, do the route in reverse, ending with a visit to Sir John Soane's Museum after 6pm, when candles augment the soft lighting of the beautiful interior – a time-capsule of 19thC London.

► STARTS
Southampton Row. Nearest tube: Holborn.

■ ENDS
Southampton Row. Nearest tube: Holborn.

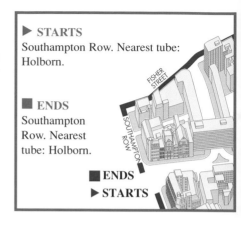

■ ENDS
► STARTS

*Interior of Sir John Soane's Museum.*

■ ENDS
► STARTS

Soane was a master of interior space, and the house seems to flow in all directions, with his use of mirrors creating a magical, labyrinthine effect.

So vast was his collection of architectural and other drawings and paintings that fold-out panels had to be fixed to the walls to hold it all. Prize of the collection is the series of Hogarth's original oils for engravings of *A Rake's Progress* and *An Election*. The house is also crammed with another phenomenal collection – broken pediment fragments, including pieces of the sarcophagus of Seti I, antique vases and an array of ancient Roman remains (open Tues-Sat 10am-5pm, lecture tour Sat, 2.30pm.)

**1** **Sir John Soane's Museum** is one of the most atmospheric small museums in London. It occupies the house the architect John Soane inhabited from 1813 to 1837 and remains virtually unchanged since then.

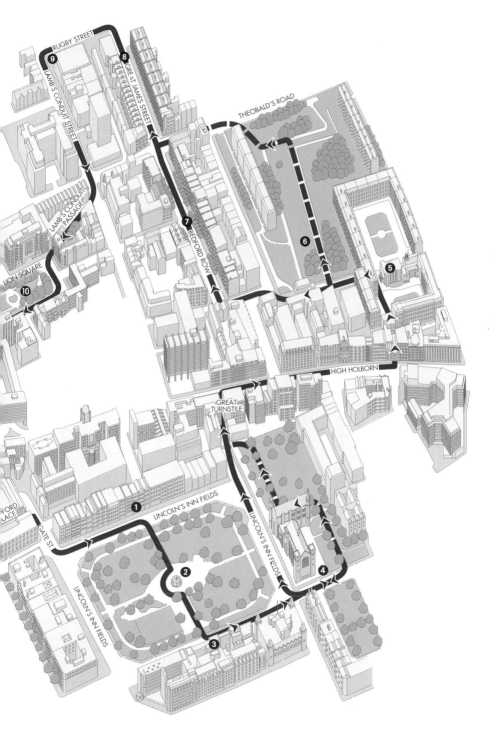

RUGBY STREET

LAMB'S CONDUIT STREET

GREAT JAMES STREET

THEOBALD'S ROAD

LAMB'S CONDUIT PASSAGE

BEDFORD ROW

...LION SQUARE

HIGH HOLBORN

GREAT TURNSTILE

...FORD ...LACE

GATE ST

LINCOLN'S INN FIELDS

LINCOLN'S INN FIELDS

LINCOLN'S INN FIELDS

*A memorial seat in Lincoln's Inn Fields.*

**2** Walk across the centre of **Lincoln's Inn Fields,** once common land grazed by cattle and now a large open space planted with plane trees. The gardens are busy on weekday lunchtimes with workers from the many nearby offices and building sites eating their sandwiches on the benches or around the bandstand. The square is lined with lawyer's chambers, among them Farrer and Co., the Queen's solicitors.

**3** On the other side of the park, at 35-43 Lincoln's Inn Fields, is the **Royal College of Surgeons of England.** Ascend its grand, frieze-lined staircase past busts and portraits of notable Fellows to the **Hunterian Museum** on the first floor. The museum is based on the collection of John Hunter, an Army surgeon from 1760 to 1763, who spent most of his time in the field treating gunshot wounds and venereal disease. At this time he began his anatomical collection with a few humble lizards. Following his return to London, Hunter's reputation as a comparative anatomist grew to such an extent that he was supplied with many rare species, including kangaroos brought back from James Cook's voyage of 1768-71. At the time of Hunter's death in 1793, there were almost 14,000 specimens in his collection. Among the museum's many fascinating exhibits is a transplanted human tooth embedded in the comb of a cockerel (open Tues-Sat 10am-5pm).

*Detail from the gate to the Royal College of Surgeons.*

**4** **Lincoln's Inn** is one of the best-looking of the Inns of Court, with its diamond-patterned brick exterior, Tudor chimneys and vaulted passageways by the chapel (the only building that it is possible to enter: open noon-2.30pm). The Inn is open on weekdays, and though it seems like a private complex of buildings, the route past the barristers' chambers, Old Hall and Great Hall is a public right of way between noon and 2.30pm. If you're here then, take a stroll through the gardens, a haven in otherwise busy Holborn. In the northwestern corner of the garden, a gateway leads out into **Great Turnstile,** an alleyway marking the original turnstile that kept in the cattle grazing on Lincoln's Inn Fields. If the gate is locked, come out of the Inn and walk to Great Turnstile via Lincoln's Inn Fields.

*Lincoln's Inn.*

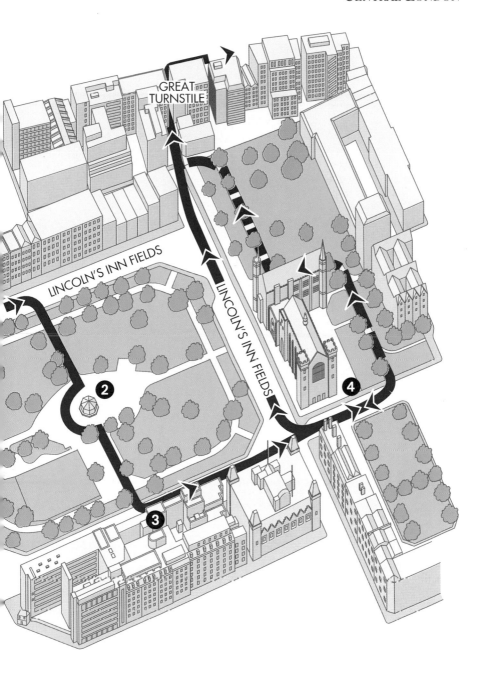

GREAT
TURNSTILE

LINCOLN'S INN FIELDS

LINCOLN'S INN FIELDS

LINCOLN'S INN FIELDS

**5** Cross High Holborn and walk to the right until you reach the Cittie of York pub, where a narrow alleyway leads through to **Gray's Inn.** Though not as good-looking as Lincoln's Inn – much of the original building was destroyed during the Blitz – the Hall does have a beautiful carved screen allegedly made of wood from a Spanish Armada ship (open by appointment only; Tel. 020 7458 7800). Shakespeare's *A Comedy of Errors* was first performed here in 1594.

*Gray's Inn.*

**6** Turn left through the archway into **Gray's Inn Gardens** (open Mon-Fri noon to 2.30pm). Back in the 17th century, the gardens became known as The Walks and were Samuel Pepys's favourite place for a stroll. Other members of society liked to take a turn here too, though not on misty mornings when bullets were flying (as The Walks was also popular with duellists). This is a peaceful lunchtime stop; the main path leads up onto Theobald's Road, but if The Walks is closed, you can reach the same point via Bedford Row.

*Silver griffin that marks the City boundary in High Holborn.*

**7** **Bedford Row** is a handsome street and one of several in the area put up by the speculative builder Nicholas Barbon. Back in the 17th century speculators built whole streets of houses as quickly as possible to create new fashionable areas. Barbon attempted this on an almost insanely grandiose scale, using dubious methods to acquire new land. Nos 36-43 are quite roughly finished but are good examples of his building style. They would originally have had wooden eaves-cornices and casement, rather than sash, windows.

**8** Continue into **Great James Street** – a beautiful example of a 1720s street where the poet Algernon Swinburne, novelist Dorothy L. Sayers and Leonard and Virginia Woolf lived at various times. At the top of Great James Street, take a quick detour to the right into Northington Street and right again into **Cockpit Yard,** a venue for cockfights in the 18th century. Fighting birds had silver spurs attached to their feet and the central area of the yard would have been covered with sand to soak up the blood. Large sums of money changed hands among the spectators, who sat in tiers of seats around the edge. When James Boswell went to a cockfight, he dressed down and left all his valuables at home. His reaction was one of pity: for the birds, who fought with 'amazing bitterness and resolution' – and for the gamblers, who seemed distracted and tense.

*High Holborn.*

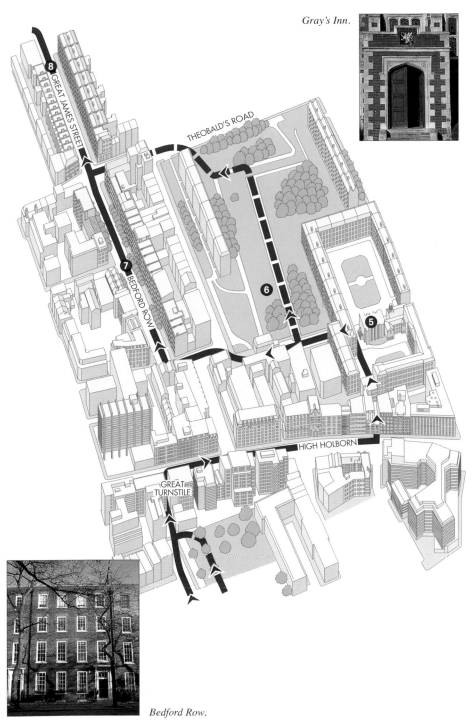

*Gray's Inn.*

GREAT JAMES STREET

8

THEOBALD'S ROAD

7

BEDFORD ROW

6

5

HIGH HOLBORN

GREAT TURNSTILE

*Bedford Row.*

**9** Retrace your steps back to Great James Street, turn right and walk up to Rugby Street. In the backyard of the former French's Dairy at No. 13, with its tiled façade, is the remains of the **White Conduit,** a vaulted underground chamber (c.1300). This chamber was originally part of a system of pipes, aqueducts and drains that channelled a fresh water supply to Greyfriars Monastery in Newgate Street and later to St Bartholomew's and Smithfield (see pages 100-107). Soon you're in thriving **Lamb's Conduit Street,** with designer shops, and its focus on art and fashion.

*Sicilian Avenue.*

At the northern end of Lamb's Conduit Street on the right (off map) is **The Lamb,** a beautiful, old-fashioned pub (though some say it's gone downhill). The modesty panels around the bar could be flipped open to buy drinks and then closed for discreet conversation, often with women of dubious reputation.

**10** Head back down Lamb's Conduit Street, cross Theobald's Road, and turn right down the pedestrianized Lamb's Conduit Passage into **Red Lion Square.** Dante Gabriel Rossetti, William Morris and Edward Burne Jones lived at No. 17 in the late 1800s. Bertrand Russell used to lecture at the Conway Hall at No. 25, home of the South Place Ethical Society which was founded in 1887.

Holborn was on the very edge of the old Italian London during the 19th century. Giuseppe Mazzini, who fought for the Unification of Italy, spent some time in political exile in London. The Mazzini and Garibaldi Club he formed in 1864, for the welfare of Italian workers in Britain, is located at No. 51. Life could be hard for immigrant workers: Mazzini went to a pawnbrokers one Saturday night to exchange his old coat and a pair of boots and found the place crowded with others doing the same thing so they could buy food for the next day.

A more flourishing representation of Italian London lies on the other side of Southampton Row. **Sicilian Avenue** (off map) was built in 1905. A short pedestrian street, it's topped and tailed by Ionic columns and finished off in red brick, white terracotta and Sicilian marble. Planters of flowers and benches are dotted along the avenue. Sit here and revive yourself, or refuel at one of the sandwich shops, the Sushi bar, or the Spaghetti House on the corner.

*Statue in Red Lion Square.*

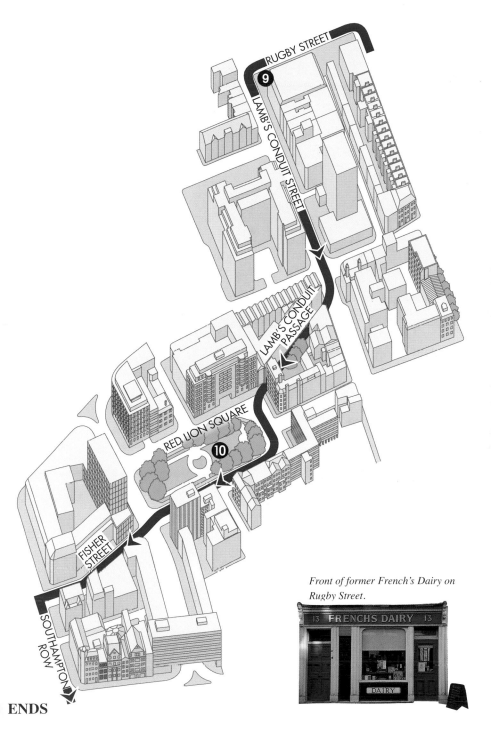

RUGBY STREET

(9)

LAMB'S CONDUIT STREET

LAMB'S CONDUIT PASSAGE

RED LION SQUARE

(10)

FISHER STREET

SOUTHAMPTON ROW

**ENDS**

*Front of former French's Dairy on
Rugby Street.*

13  FRENCH'S DAIRY  13

DAIRY

# Smithfield

*Smithfield Market Coat of Arms.*

S mithfield market was once so busy that a bypass route was built around London (now the Euston Road) so the cattle being driven to market didn't block up Oxford Street. Meat is still traded here, but the area has undergone a renaissance and the market has been revamped. Today this area is to the City what Soho and Covent Garden are to the West End, with plenty of clubs, bars and restaurants. These and the media-linked businesses that have moved into the area have brought in new wealth – in the last century Clerkenwell and neighbouring Holborn were the poorest districts in London. The most remarkable part of Smithfield, however, is the oldest. The Priory church and hospital of St Bartholomew date back to the 12th century and the mainly Norman church is one of the most atmospheric in London. This is one walk in particular which gives a vivid impression of the past.

▶ **STARTS**
❶

■ **ENDS**

COWCROSS STREET

BENJAMIN STREET

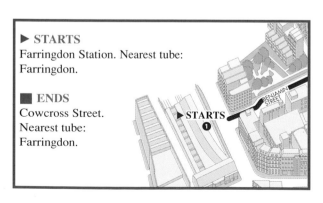

▶ **STARTS**
Farringdon Station. Nearest tube: Farringdon.

■ **ENDS**
Cowcross Street. Nearest tube: Farringdon.

▶ STARTS
❶

BENJAMIN STREET

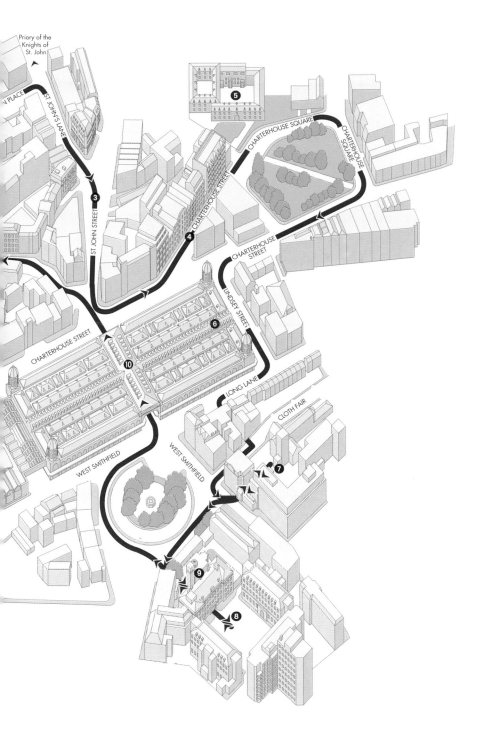

Priory of the
Knights of
St. John

N PLACE

ST JOHN'S LANE

**5**

CHARTERHOUSE STREET

CHARTERHOUSE SQUARE

CHARTERHOUSE SQUARE

**3**

ST JOHN STREET

**4**

CHARTERHOUSE STREET

CHARTERHOUSE STREET

LINDSEY STREET

**6**

CHARTERHOUSE STREET

**10**

LONG LANE

CLOTH FAIR

**7**

WEST SMITHFIELD

WEST SMITHFIELD

**9**

**8**

**❶ Farringdon Station** (1863) was the original terminus of the Metropolitan line, the world's first underground railway. Between the Wars, overground extensions were built between the City and the newly fashionable leafy suburb of Hertfordshire, known as Metroland. Its golf courses, clean air and open fields, conveniently close to town, were keenly promoted by the railway companies wanting to build up a profitable commuter trade.

*Innovative architecture abounds around Smithfield, such as this house by Piers Gough.*

STARTS ❶

BENJAMIN STREET

**❷** This area has always had its own more chancy identity, free from the jurisdiction of the Guilds that controlled trade within the City walls. **Farringdon** now marks the gateway to Media- rather than Metroland: these days it's frequented by young turks from internet consultancies, journalists from the *Guardian* and *Observer,* and a sprinkling of club kids, dancing queens, and Suits from the City, all seeking out its upscale restaurants and bars. On the corner of Benjamin Street and Britton Street, media doyenne Janet Street-Porter's house, with its innovative blue pitched roof, was designed by Piers Gough in 1987. Jibby Beane, the artworld entrepreneur, has her space at 66 St John Street, nearby.

**❸** As you walk along St John's Lane, notice the imposing gateway visible further up the street which belonged to the **Priory of the Knights of St John** before the Dissolution of the Monasteries. Head south and join **St John Street,** the old drovers' route for animals heading for Smithfield market, which once had 23 pubs along its route. The watering holes here now are strictly fashionable. **Tinseltown** at No. 44 (Tel. 020 7689 2424) is an American café open 24 hours a day. (Owner Sheeraz says he goes to Los Angeles every six weeks "to check out the trends"). **Vic Naylor's,** a couple of doors down at Nos 38-40, is packed

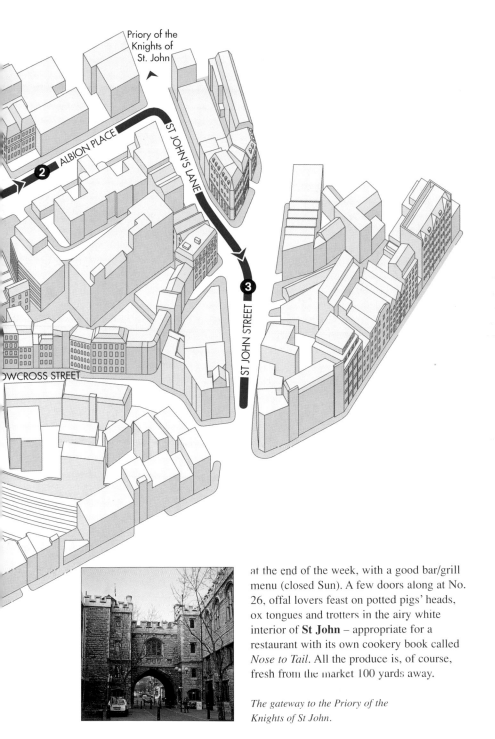

Priory of the
Knights of
St. John

ALBION PLACE

ST JOHN'S LANE

ST JOHN STREET

OWCROSS STREET

at the end of the week, with a good bar/grill menu (closed Sun). A few doors along at No. 26, offal lovers feast on potted pigs' heads, ox tongues and trotters in the airy white interior of **St John** – appropriate for a restaurant with its own cookery book called *Nose to Tail*. All the produce is, of course, fresh from the market 100 yards away.

*The gateway to the Priory of the Knights of St John.*

❹ The route now cuts through to Charterhouse Street where the **Fox and Anchor** is located (with a beautiful 1898 façade). It has an early licence allowing it to open at 7am. Butchers, carmen, porters and anyone with business at the market can drink and have breakfast here. These days, however, early-rising City workers account for much of the custom. Further along the street at Nos. 61-63 is **Le Comptoir,** a deli by day and an excellent restaurant specialising in the cooking of South West France by night, at reasonable prices (Tel. 020 7608 0851).

❺ **Charterhouse** refers to the beautiful complex of buildings flanking the square, which stand on the site of a 14thC Carthusian monastery. After Dissolution, Charterhouse became a school and then a hospice. It's now home to Charterhouse pensioners and the grounds are closed to the public except for guided tours (£10, Tel. 0207 251 5002), or for Sunday services at 9.45am and 5.45pm in the Charterhouse chapel.

❻ The walk skirts Smithfield market (now renamed **Central Markets**), gleaming in its newly restored colours, with the dragon slayed by St George guarding the main avenues. The building, designed by Horace Jones, went up in 1868 with the imposing green-domed towers on each corner originally designed as on-site pubs. The name Smithfields comes from 'smoothfields.' In the 12th century this open space (close to the

*Smithfield Market detail.*

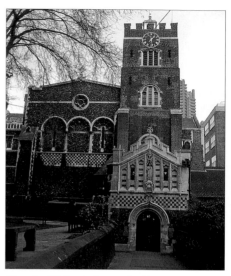

*Church of St Bartholomew-the-Great.*

City) was used for horsefairs, jousting, tournaments, executions and, above all, for Bartholomew Fair. This rowdy, popular event (immortalized in Ben Jonson's 17thC play of the same name) was eventually shut down in 1855 by the authorities who were worried that it had got too out of hand.

❼ The passageways around **Cloth Fair** are narrow and atmospheric, giving an idea of what medieval London was like. In the middle of them is hidden the church of **St Bartholomew-the-Great,** founded as a Priory in 1123. Rahere, a court-jester to Henry I, built the church to fulfil a vow he made when he closely avoided death from malaria on a pilgrimage to Rome. The Priory was connected with St Bartholomew's Hospital, an infirmary which took in travellers, the sick, the aged and the destitute. The church is full of shadows and flickering candlelight. Rahere's tomb is set into the wall (he's the one lying on a pillow with his hands in the prayer position, underneath three arches), one of the few dimly lit features. The church dates from Norman times – most of the arches are

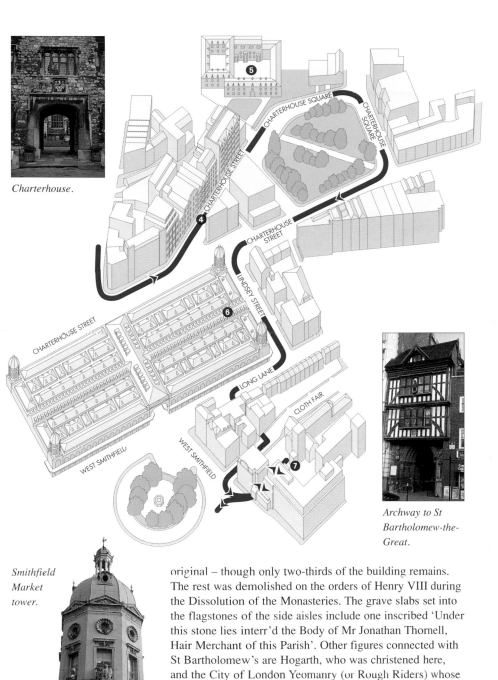

*Charterhouse.*

*Archway to St Bartholomew-the-Great.*

*Smithfield Market tower.*

original – though only two-thirds of the building remains. The rest was demolished on the orders of Henry VIII during the Dissolution of the Monasteries. The grave slabs set into the flagstones of the side aisles include one inscribed 'Under this stone lies interr'd the Body of Mr Jonathan Thornell, Hair Merchant of this Parish'. Other figures connected with St Bartholomew's are Hogarth, who was christened here, and the City of London Yeomanry (or Rough Riders) whose ceremonial drums are on display.
(Open Tues-Fri 8.30am-4pm; Sat 10.30am-1.30pm; Sun 8.30am-1pm, 2.30pm-8pm.)

*The courtyard of St Bartholomew's Hospital, a fine example (1730-59) of the work of architect James Gibb.*

**8** By 1150 St Bartholomew's had become known as a place of refuge for those seeking miraculous cures. Today **St Bartholomew's Hospital,** better known as Bart's, is one of London's best-loved hospitals, and some would say a miraculous survivor itself – of cutbacks and threats of closure. In its early days the hospital was one of the few places that took in foundlings, orphans and babies from Newgate prison nearby (see page 114). Others sought safety there too: a copy of an 18thC engraving in the hospital museum (open Tues-Fri 10am-4pm) shows Wat Tyler, leader of the Peasant's Revolt (1381) being dragged out of the hospital where he had been treated for stab wounds before being taken off to be executed. The museum also contains some worrying early medical instruments that make one glad to have been born in the late 20th century, and exhibits on the experience of women at the medical school. On the grand staircase leading to the hospital's Great Hall, two stairwell-high paintings by William Hogarth show variously injured, pale, sick and bandaged figures.

**9** Just before the entrance to the museum is the church of **St Bartholomew-the-Lesser,** a light, business-like place compared with the Great. A stained-glass panel here (1950) depicts Rahere in monk's robes but with one leg in jester's stockings and a pompom shoe poking out. Rahere kneels with his arms outstretched next to St Bartholomew himself, with a flaying knife – the gruesome instrument of his martyrdom – held high.

**10** Perhaps it's not appropriate, after all this talk of martyrdom and operations, to take a trip through the meat market. All the

*Detail from Smithfield Market Entrance.*

trading is over by 8am, however, and a stroll along the main avenue will not upset the squeamish (though strict vegetarians probably won't be keen).

Public executions were once held in the market itself, and scenes of hanging, disembowelling and torture were commonplace. Indeed it was here that William Wallace (who led Scotland during the Wars of Independence) met his famous end: following his trial in 1305 he was hung, drawn and quartered on the site.

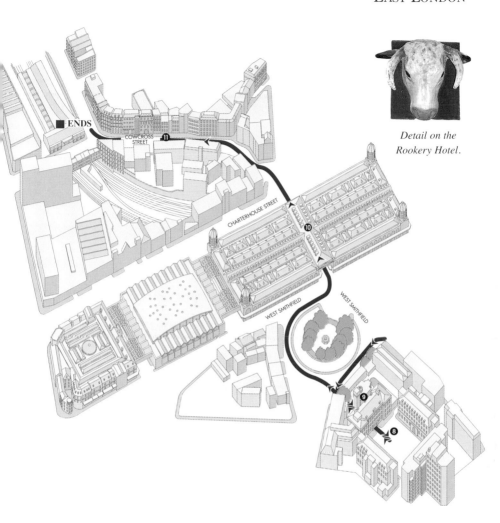

Detail on the
Rookery Hotel.

**11 Cowcross Street** leads back to Farringdon Station, with **The Hope** pub (and Sir Loin restaurant above) being one of the first of many bars and restaurants you'll pass on this strip. Sir Loin, so the story goes, is the correct way to spell this cut of meat, since the time when James I, so pleased with a steak served up to him, decided to knight it. You can ponder on the truth of this if you succumb to the full English breakfast served here. Across the road, on the corner of Peter Lane and Cowcross Street, is the small, Georgian-style hotel **The Rookery** (with the cow weather vane on its roof). This whole area was known as The Rookery in the 19th century, when it was one of the worst slum areas in London – a world away from its current happening, up-and-come identity.

# St Paul's

▶ STARTS

Cheapside. Nearest tube: Bank.

The concentration of banks and the business-like crowds give the 'square mile' of the City a completely different atmosphere from the West End, with the streets off Cheapside as busy as they were in medieval times, when this was the commercial heart of London. Their names – Poultry, Bread, Milk Street and Ironmongers Lane – show what used to be on sale. Rising above it all, St Paul's Cathedral is a landmark sight in a sea of office blocks, connected to The Tate Modern art gallery on the other side of the river (across the delicate span of Norman Foster's Millennium Bridge). Also on the walk are the Old Bailey, where some of Britain's grisliest crimes have been brought to trial; Fleet Street, whose association with the printing industry dates back to William Caxton, and some of Christopher Wren's most beautiful churches, rebuilt after the devastating Great Fire of 1666.

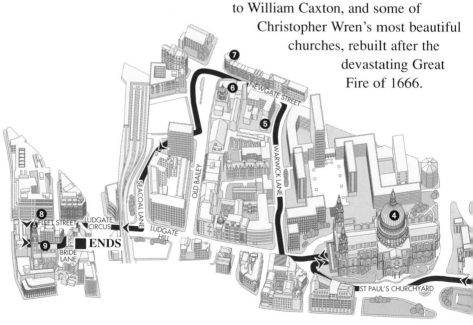

*St Paul's Cathedral,
designed by Christopher
Wren in the classical style of
ancient Greece and Rome.*

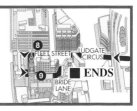

■ **ENDS**
Fleet Street.
Nearest tube: St
Paul's.

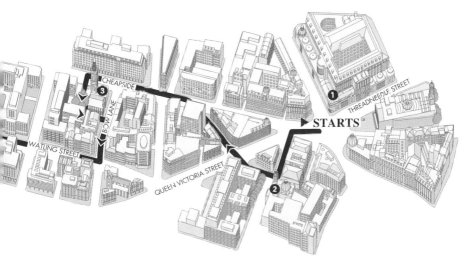

**1** London is one of the busiest financial markets in the world, with most of the trading taking place in the 'square mile' around the **Bank of England.** The Bank's museum on Bartholomew Street gives the full story and offers the chance to play at trading on interactive displays in a recreation of the stock office designed by John Soane in 1793 (museum open Tues-Sat, 10am-5pm; free). Though it's not clearly defined, the 'square mile' is roughly based on the land that lay within the city walls where thousands of craftsmen, apprentices, merchants and their families lived in the middle ages. Most of the area burned down in the Great Fire of 1666 and though the original wooden houses were lost, the churches rebuilt by Christopher Wren are magnificent.

**2** In the heart of the City, a few steps from the Bank of England, is **St Stephen Walbrook,** the Lord Mayor of London's parish church. It's one of Wren's best buildings: airy and beautiful, and topped by a dome. The white stone

*Church of St Stephen Walbrook by Christopher Wren.*

*Bank of England Museum.*

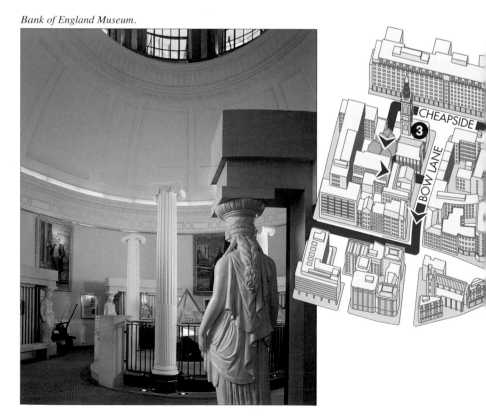

altar by Henry Moore (1987) makes a contemporary foil for the dark, decorative pulpit and font.

❸ Another Wren church is **St Mary-le-Bow** on Cheapside, whose bell is the 'great bell of Bow' from the nursery rhyme 'Oranges and Lemons.' Tradition says that to be born within earshot of the Bow Bells gives you the right to call yourself a true Cockney. The interior of the church is fairly plain - for atmosphere head to the vaulted Norman crypt where there's a bustling restaurant, open at lunchtime. On Tuesdays there are regular 'lunchtime dialogues' between the Rector in one pulpit and a guest in the other – in the past these guests have ranged from actors to the governor of the Bank of England.

*St Mary-le-Bow on Cheapside.*

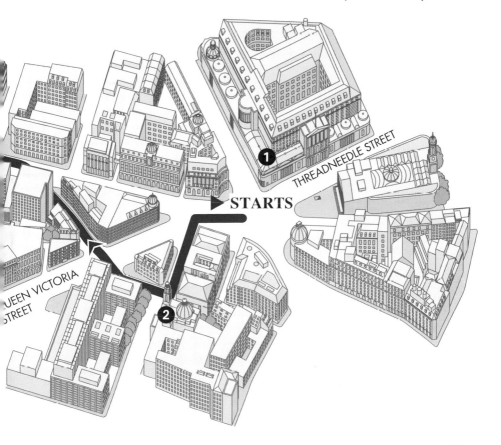

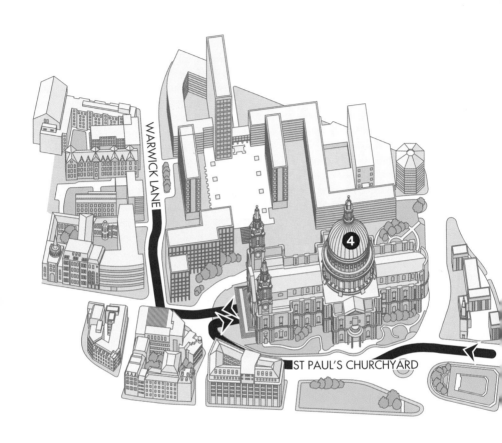

WARWICK LANE

■ST PAUL'S CHURCHYARD

**4** Zig-zag through the back streets of Bow Lane and Watling Street (an old Roman road) to **St Paul's.** There has been a cathedral on this site since Norman times, when it was the largest in northern Europe. Christopher Wren's cathedral, completed in 1710, was supposed to have a spire like its predecessor. During construction, however, Wren hid the top of the new cathedral under scaffolding and sneaked in a dome more in keeping with the baroque style of his design.

The monumental interior has some highlights, such as the choir stalls and organ case by the master woodcarver Grinling Gibbons, or William Holman Hunt's painting *The Light of the World* (c. 1900). But it's as a venue for state occasions that St Paul's has excelled. Monarchs have held their Jubilee services in the cathedral, and their offspring have married here. In 1852, thousands crammed in for the

*Memorial to the fire-watchers who kept a nightly vigil during the Blitz (1940-1).*

funeral of the Duke of Wellington when the interior was draped in black cloth and lit for the first time by gas lights. In 1806, Admiral Nelson's funeral cortège travelled by barge up the Thames to St Paul's, his body preserved in brandy by the crew of HMS Victory. His tomb, along with that of Wellington, is in the crypt.

A favourite destination for children (and others) is the **Whispering Gallery,** where the quirky acoustics mean that someone with their ear close to the wall on one side of the dome can just about hear what you say on the other. There are usually a few people trying this out after clambering up the 259 stairs. More steps lead up to the **Stone Gallery** (53m and 378 steps high) and the smaller

**Golden Gallery** (85m and 530 steps above ground level). Just how difficult it was for the painters and mosaic artists to work at this height is clear from a story about James Thornhill, responsible for the paintings of St Paul on the inside of the dome. Thornhill's life was saved one day by an assistant who, when he saw that the painter was in imminent danger of stepping backwards off their wooden platform, spoilt the work so that Thornhill would lunge forward to stop the damage and save himself from falling to his death.

*Right: Queen Anne, monarch when St Paul's was completed, stands near the entrance.*

*Above: The Lovers, next to St Paul's Cathedral.*

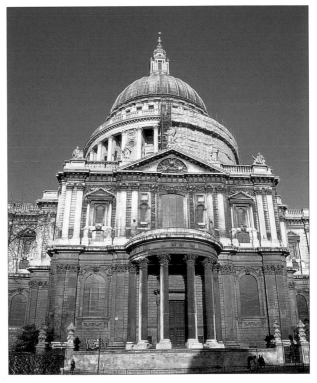

*Right: the south side of St Paul's, from St Paul's Churchyard.*

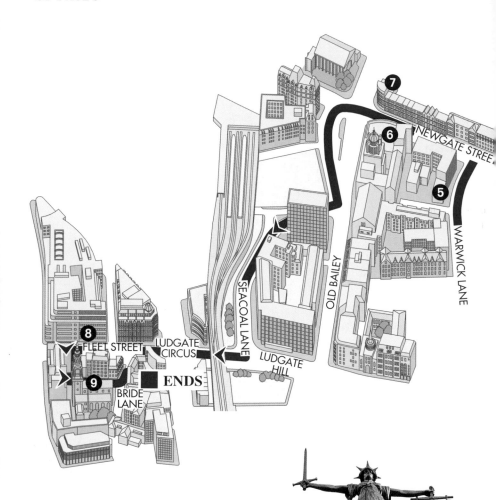

**5** A right turn from in front of the cathedral takes you up Ave Maria lane and into Warwick Lane, past **Stationers' Hall** and **Cutlers' Hall.** Notice the long terracotta frieze of cutlery makers pounding metal, working bellows for their furnace, and sitting at grinding wheels. Walk up Warwick Lane until it opens out onto **Newgate Street** – this road is named after the huge prison built here in the 12th century which finally closed in 1880.

*The bronze figure of Justice on the dome of the Old Bailey.*

**6** **The Old Bailey,** Britain's premier court, has a certain macabre interest. It stands on the site of Newgate prison and the old west gate of the Roman city, with stones from Newgate going into the construction of the Edwardian baroque building (1902-7). Its 19 courts handle around 1,700 cases a year. In its time the Old Bailey has attracted 'the most notorious of criminals, the most odious of crimes'. The public galleries are open from 10.30am until 1pm, and again 2pm until the courts rise at around 5pm. On the first two days of each session, judges carry posies of flowers as a reminder of the days when they counteracted the stink of the fumes that caused gaol fever.

**7** Across the road, **The Viaduct Tavern** on Newgate Street is a wonderful example of a Victorian gin palace. It opened in 1869, the same year that Queen Victoria opened the Holborn Viaduct. Inside, paintings of three languid female figures represent agriculture, the arts and banking – the middle with a tear in it from when a soldier during the First World War charged at it with his bayonet. The beautiful copper ceiling is supported by a cast-iron column, and the chubby, black-haired stone relief faces around the walls just below cornice level are said to represent the sixteen 'hanging' judges of the Old Bailey across the road.

**8** Ludgate Circus marks the beginning of **Fleet Street,** or the Street of Shame as the satirical magazine *Private Eye* refers to it. It was long the home of Britain's national newspapers before they moved away in the 1980s. The first number of the *Sunday Times* was edited just off Fleet Street on Salisbury Court on 20th October 1822, and the **Punch Tavern** (look out for the golden face of Mr Punch on the pub sign) on Fleet Street was where the magazine of the same name was planned in 1841. One news agency – Reuters – has stayed: the façade of their monumental building by Lutyens (1935) shows a larger-than-life figure trumpeting news across the globe.

**9** Fleet Street and publishing go back here further than the 19th century: Wynkyn de Worde brought the first printing press to the City in 1500. He set it up in the local church of **St Bride's,** now known as the Printers Cathedral or the Journalists Church. Wren designed the present St Bride's in 1703, thoughtfully building the Old Bell Inn nearby at the same time for the stonemasons. The church's five-tiered spire may look familiar – millions of wedding cakes have been based on it, after a Fleet Street pastry cook, Mr Rich, first copied it in the 18th century.

*Tavern named after the nearby Holborn Viaduct.*

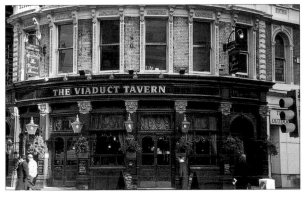

# Tower of London

This walk can take the whole day if you choose to go inside the Tower of London, the Tower Bridge Experience and the Design Museum (then have lunch at St Katharine's Dock and dinner at Butler's Wharf). Or it can be a shorter walk of a couple of hours

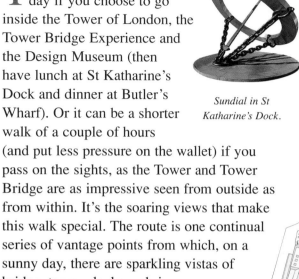

*Sundial in St Katharine's Dock.*

(and put less pressure on the wallet) if you pass on the sights, as the Tower and Tower Bridge are as impressive seen from outside as from within. It's the soaring views that make this walk special. The route is one continual series of vantage points from which, on a sunny day, there are sparkling vistas of bridge, tower, docks and river.

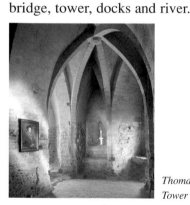

*Thomas More's cell in the Tower of London.*

▶ **STARTS**
Tower Hill. Nearest tube: Tower Hill.

◼ **ENDS**
Tower Bridge. Nearest tube: Tower Hill.

*War memorial on pillars at Tower Hill.*

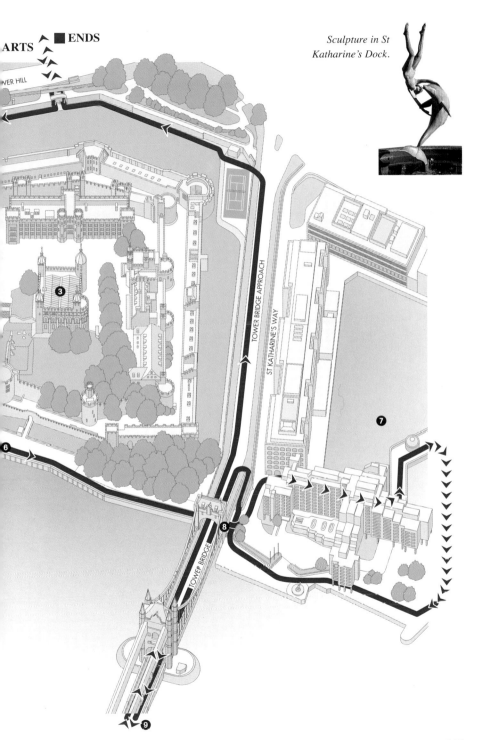

ARTS ▲ ■ ENDS

TOWER HILL

*Sculpture in St Katharine's Dock.*

TOWER BRIDGE APPROACH

ST KATHARINE'S WAY

TOWER BRIDGE

❸

❻

❼

❽

❾

**1** Exit from the tube and walk up the steps to the **viewpoint** and giant sundial. A panoramic strip is labelled with the names of all the neighbouring buildings. Among the grandest is **Trinity Square,** formerly the Port of London Authority headquarters (designed by Edwin Cooper, 1912-22), set up to regulate the dock companies and the 100,000 men who worked for them at the beginning of the 20th century. River trade has been important to London since Roman times: a stretch of Roman Wall (containing medieval parts) which protected the City is visible next to the tube station.

All this land once lay within the bounds of the Tower Liberty – in 1687 anyone living within the Liberty was free from the laws of the City of London. Though the Liberty charter was dissolved in 1894, the beating of the bounds still takes place every third year on Ascension Day. On this day, boys who have a family connection with the Tower are given white wands and led around the boundary by the Tower Chaplain, who proclaims at every boundary mark: "Cursed is he who removeth his neighbour's landmark." When the Chief Warder orders "Whack it, boys, whack it", the boys duly beat the boundary with their wands – it's one way of remembering where a boundary lies.

**2** Walk back down to the tube entrance and follow the signs through the underpass to the **Tower of London.** The route splits off to the right; take this path around the edge of the moat and you will find the Tower ticket office. If you don't want to go into the Tower, exit on to Tower Hill at this point and gain free access via the entrance for cars to **The Wharf,** the waterfront path leading between the Tower and the river.

From a distance you get an impression of how impregnable the Tower was and it comes as

*The White Tower.*

no surprise to learn that very few prisoners held here ever escaped. For Londoners, the tower has symbolized very different things throughout its history. It was built by the conquering Normans (completed by 1290) as a fortress, a symbol of domination. Later it became a place of refuge: London's Jews found shelter from rioting mobs many times during the 13th century. The Constable of the Tower of London administered justice from here and imprisoned anyone suspected of tax evasion in the Tower. The Yeomen of the Guard (Beefeaters) have become an icon of Englishness. Mosley led his Blackshirts from the Tower – an evocative meeting point – through the Jewish East End in 1936.

*A Yeoman Warder.*

**3** The **White Tower** is the most recognizable part of the Tower of London, a stronghold dating from the 11th century with walls 15 ft (4.6 m) thick. It was begun by William the Conqueror and finished by his son William II, though it was William II's brother Henry I who started using the stone apartments as a prison. The White Tower has had many roles: inside is the **Chapel of St John**

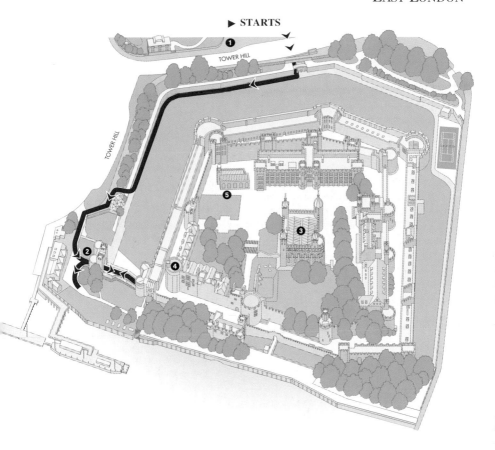

the Evangelist, a circular space lined with rows of Norman arches. Here young noblemen in the day of Henry IV, after ritual bathing, would keep overnight vigil before being knighted the next day.

❹ The majority of the towers were used by various monarchs over the years to imprison those who threatened their power. Thomas More, Henry VIII's Chancellor and chief political advisor, was imprisoned in a small stone dungeon in the lower part of the Bell Tower. He refused to swear allegiance to Henry VIII as Head of the Church in England in place of the Pope. The cell where he was held captive for 15 months (from 17 April 1534) was opened to the public for the first time to mark the year 2000. More was

beheaded on Tower Hill in 1535.

❺ Thomas More's head was displayed on London Bridge to deter others from objecting to the King's divorce from Catherine of Aragon. Some say the head was retrieved by his daughter Margaret and later buried in Canterbury by his son-in-law. His body, like those of the hundreds of others who were beheaded at the scaffold, was buried in the Chapel of St Peter ad Vincula (St Peter in chains), which still stands within the tower walls.

**6** **Traitor's Gate** has its dark, dank entrance next to The Wharf. State prisoners would arrive by barge at the Tower from the law courts at Westminster to the oak and iron gates in the base of St Thomas's Tower – a forbidding sight. **The Wharf** separates the moat from the river. On the opposite bank is the battle cruiser HMS Belfast. Launched in 1938 and still bristling with guns, it's the only surviving ship from the great fleets of armoured warships built for the Royal Navy in the early 20th century (open 10am-5pm or 6pm). **City Hall,** the striking rounded glass building that stands on the opposite bank, is the Mayor of London's headquarters.

**7** Walk under the archway into **St Katharine's Dock** (1828) along the path to the left of the Thistle Tower Hotel. Signs point towards Ivory House, built in 1854 to store ivory, perfume, wine, shells and other precious cargo. Among the buildings on the landward side are the modern World Trade Centre and the London Fox Futures and Options Exchange, which deals in coffee, cocoa and sugar. Though once a busy dock for shipping, trade here declined in the years following the Second World War and in the 1970s the wharves and basins were converted into a yacht marina with shops, pubs and cafés. Old Thames sailing barges moor up alongside the jetties and yachts come through the lock, with its 9-10m drop, when the tide is up.

**8** Follow the riverside path back to Tower Bridge and past **Dead Man's Hole,** where bodies from the Tower were retrieved from the water and stored in the mortuary below. A sign points you in the direction of the **Tower Bridge Experience,** which gives access to the high-level walkways and to a museum. The path across the bridge also affords superb views of London, with the vast Victorian warehouses of Butler's Wharf downriver, and St Paul's and the gold-topped column

*St Katharine's Dock.*

Monument marking the spot where the Great Fire of London started in 1666. The steel-framed bridge (1894) was high-tech for its time, a superb example of Victorian engineering by John Wolfe-Barry. The architect, Horace Jones, called his bridge "steel skeletons clothed with stone" and his ghostly presence leads visitors through the 'Experience'.

**8** The **bridge** opens for ships around 500 times a year – you can see the break in the road where the two halves join, the bascules now raised by electric power rather than the original steam-driven system of hydraulics. It's a spectacular sight, though not so enjoyable if you are stuck on the wrong side and have to wait for the bridge to go down again. The engine rooms are on the south bank, opposite the Tower. Peer through the window next to the entrance for an idea of the scale and weight of the pistons and cogs that drove the engines until 1976. In more than 80 years they never once broke down.

*Tower Bridge.*

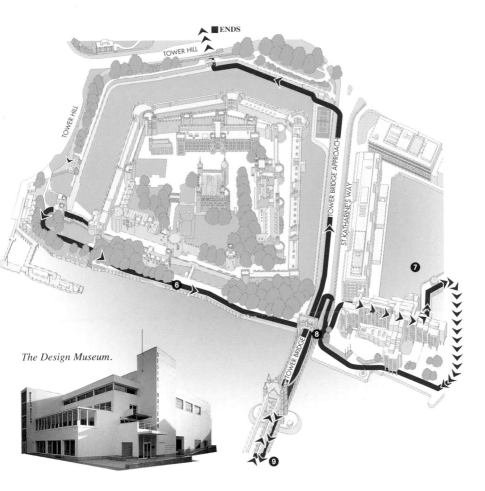

*The Design Museum.*

**9** The narrow street leading away from the base of Tower Bridge is called **Shad Thames** (just off map). Its unique criss-cross construction high above the street dates from the days when tea and spices were unloaded into Butler's Wharf and then transferred by porters into warehouses behind. Many of the warehouses have been turned into loft apartments, but the names of the streets and buildings are a reminder of exotic 19thC cargoes and far-off ports. Keep walking to the end of Shad Thames and the **Design Museum,** a showcase for 20thC design with the highly praised **Blueprint Café** next door. Outside the museum are a huge bronze head

by Eduardo Paolozzi (1989) and benches overlooking the river. One of Terence Conran's restaurants along the Thames Path between here and Tower Bridge would be an excellent place to stop for lunch or dinner – the **Pont de la Tour** (where in the late 1990s the Blairs took the Clintons for a casual 'state' dinner); the cheaper **Cantina** or the **Butler's Wharf Chop House.**

To return to Tower Hill, walk back along the Thames Path to Tower Bridge and cross the river. Steps lead down to a park by the Tower of London moat, which takes you back to Tower Hill tube station.

# Greenwich

Cutty Sark Gardens.
Nearest Docklands Light
Railway station: Cutty
Sark. Nearest rail sta-
tion: Greenwich (served
by trains from Charing
Cross, Waterloo East and
London Bridge).
If you arrive by river
boat or Docklands
Light Railway you will
emerge right outside the
Cutty Sark and the start
of this walk.
Alternatively, you could
emerge from the
Greenwich Foot Tunnel
which runs under the
Thames from Island
Gardens (DLR station).
If arriving by rail, turn
left out of Greenwich
station and walk down
Greenwich High Street,
following the arrows to
the Cutty Sark.

■ ENDS

Cutty Sark Gardens.
Nearest transport: as
above.

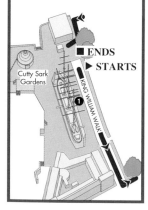

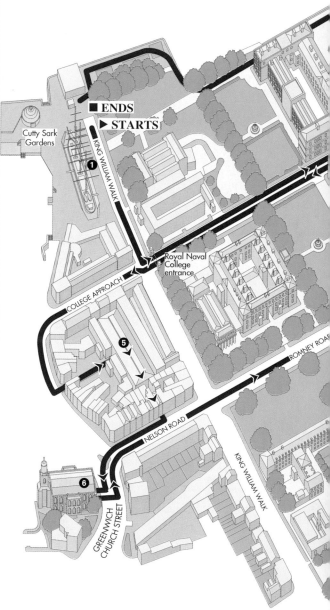

122

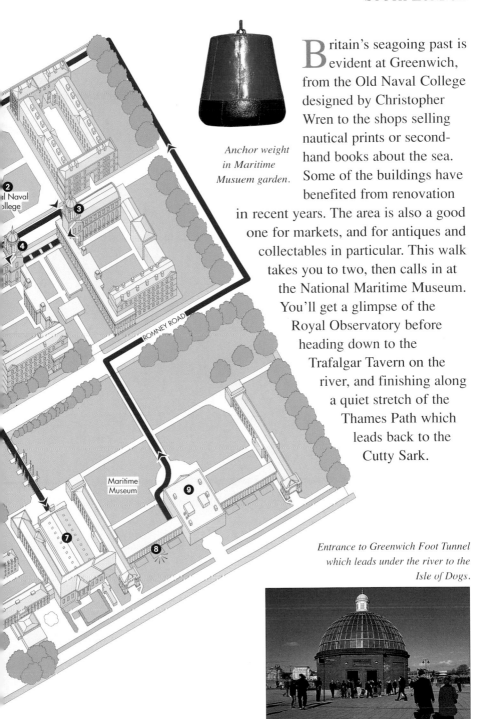

*Anchor weight in Maritime Musuem garden.*

Britain's seagoing past is evident at Greenwich, from the Old Naval College designed by Christopher Wren to the shops selling nautical prints or second-hand books about the sea. Some of the buildings have benefited from renovation in recent years. The area is also a good one for markets, and for antiques and collectables in particular. This walk takes you to two, then calls in at the National Maritime Museum. You'll get a glimpse of the Royal Observatory before heading down to the Trafalgar Tavern on the river, and finishing along a quiet stretch of the Thames Path which leads back to the Cutty Sark.

*Entrance to Greenwich Foot Tunnel which leads under the river to the Isle of Dogs.*

*Cutty Sark.*

❶ A tea clipper built in 1869, the **Cutty Sark** served the China tea trade (1870-77) and then the Australian wool trade (1883-95) and is still permeated by the smoky smell of Lapsang Souchong. Her decks – originally manned by a crew of 28 – and her dark wooden cargo holds are wonderfully evocative. (Open daily 10am-5pm.)

The **Gypsy Moth** nearby was built for yachtsman Francis Chichester to test whether a yacht of modern design could compete with the speed of the old racing clippers. Chichester sailed her single-handedly around the world in 1966-7, and set many records, including 1,400 miles sailed in eight days. The Cutty Sark, however, remained the faster ship, her record being 363 miles sailed in a single day.

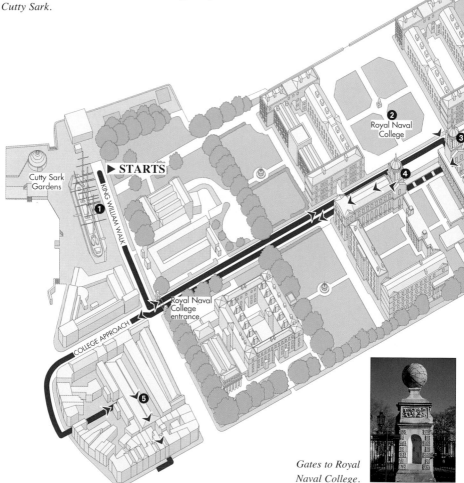

*Gates to Royal Naval College.*

**2** A few steps away from the river is the side entrance of the **Old Royal Naval Hospital** (the grand entrance is reserved for state occasions). This site was originally the location of the Tudor Greenwich Palace, a favourite of Henry VIII and his daughters Mary and Elizabeth. Later, William and Mary decamped to Hampton Court where the air was healthier, and a home for disabled seamen was built on this site. Christopher Wren planned the complex and, during the first half of the 18th century, Hawksmoor and Vanbrugh were among the architects who finished off his grand scheme.

**3** The complex became the **Royal Naval College** (open 10am-5pm) from 1873-1998. A stroll through the gates brings you to the College's farthest dome, under which is the **Georgian Chapel** (1789). The interior is like a beautifully crafted piece of Wedgwood. Everything is lovingly made, from the restrained curve and sinuous steps of the wooden pulpit to the marble floor with its anchor, compass and rope border.

**4** A spiral stone staircase and underground passage known as Chalk Walk (book in advance: Tel. 020 8269 4791) leads to the other dome, and the College's **Painted Hall** (1727). The walls and ceilings in this opulent dining hall are decorated with a host of figures – all sprawling limbs and billowing robes – celebrating Britain's Protestant monarchy. The room is still used for banquets: diners are seated under the large central oval of the ceiling, where Peace hands an olive branch to William, while Concord attends Queen Mary.

*Royal Naval College.*

**5** Exit the Naval College the way you came in and cross the road into College Approach. Among several small shops is **Decomania** at No. 9, which specializes in fine art deco furniture and *objets d'art*. The **Greenwich Market** has its entrance on Greenwich Church Street, and sells a mixture of wares from Fifties treasures to contemporary glassware, with a sprinkling of street fashion, jewellery, knick-knacks and food.

*Thirties collectables at Decomania.*

**6** Further up Greenwich Church Street, the grimy, patched-up exterior of the Church of **St Alfege's** gives nothing away about its past. On this site Alfege, the Archbishop of Canterbury, was martyred by Viking raiders in 1012 and Henry VIII was baptized in 1491. The present church, designed by Hawksmoor and dedicated in 1718, suffered much bomb damage in World War II. Cross Greenwich Church Street here and head along **Nelson Road,** lined with shops selling model ships, TexMex food and second-hand books.

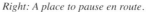

*Left: St Alfege's.*

*Right: A place to pause en route.*

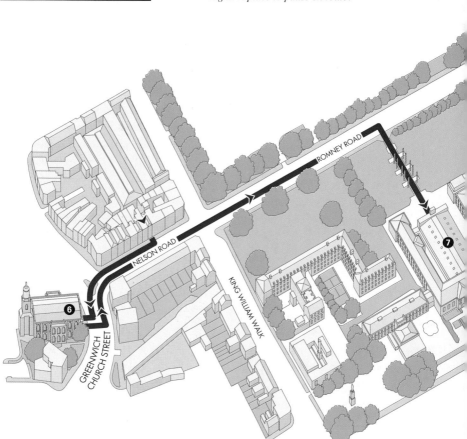

**7** The entrance to the **National Maritime Museum** is on Romney Road; remodelled in 1999, the museum is lively and entertaining. Among the many exhibits is the steam-driven engine from the paddle tug *Reliant,* which moves with balletic calm in the light-filled main gallery. Experience life on board on a variety of vessels, from a naval submarine to a mammoth passenger liner of the Thirties.

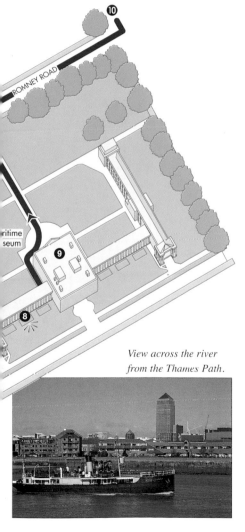

*View across the river from the Thames Path.*

**8** The loggia between the Maritime Museum and the Queen's House gives a stately view of **Greenwich Park** (landscaped by Le Nôtre in the reign of Charles II) and the **Royal Observatory.** Well worth the climb for its stunning views over London, the Royal Observatory is the location of the meridian line marking the juncture between eastern and western hemispheres.

Captain James Cook

*Statue to the explorer Captain Cook in Greenwich Park.*

**9** The **Queen's House** is a perfect Palladian villa (the first in England) designed by Inigo Jones and completed in 1638 for Henrietta Maria, daughter-in-law of James I. The plans for the Naval College were changed at her request: the single domed palace – which would have blocked her view – was abandoned in favour of two separate domed buildings with a vista of river in between. (The Maritime Museum, including the Royal Observatory and the Queen's House, is open 10am-5pm.)

**10** A quiet stretch of the **Thames Path** flanks the grand façade of the Royal Naval College and ends this walk. After leaving the Queen's House, turn right then take your first left, skirting the Naval College (now the University of Greenwich and the Trinity College of Music). This brings you to the **Trafalgar Tavern,** where Dickens, Wilkie Collins and Thackeray used to meet for a drink, and where Dickens set the wedding feast in *Our Mutual Friend.* From here you get a clear view along the river to the **Millennium Dome** before the stone flagged pavement – splashed by the occasional wake of a passing boat – leads you back to Greenwich Pier.

**Celia Woolfrey** is a journalist, writing for news stand magazines and book publishers. She loves walking – in mountainous terrain as well as around cities – and thinks the best way to see London is on foot.